Classic Tales
In
California
History

Alton Pryor

Classic Tales
In
California History

Alton Pryor

Stagecoach Publishing
Roseville, California
www.stagecoachpublishing.com
stagecoach@surewest.net

Classic Tales
In
California History

ISBN: 978-0-9660053-2-5
Library of Congress Catalog Card Number: 99-90714

Stagecoach
Publishing
5360 Campcreek Loop
Roseville, CA. 95747
Phone (916) 771-8166
E:mail: stagecoach@surewest.net
www.stagecoachpublishing.com

Table of Contents

Always read something that will make you look good if you die in the middle of it.   P.J. O'Rourke

Chapter 1

America's Only Emperor

Joshua Norton was San Francisco's curiosity for years.

Joshua Abraham Norton was a picturesque figure and the citizens of San Francisco adopted and gave him the royal treatment he demanded. Norton, you see, proclaimed himself Norton I, Emperor of the United States and Protector of Mexico. The peculiar Norton was one of California's most colorful figures, although few history books mention him. Little is known about him. He was born about 1818 in London, England, but grew up in South Africa where his parents went to seek their fortune.

"The Emperor further orders that anyone posting this defamatory picture of himself with the two vile curs known as Bummer and Lazarus shall add the following disclaimer: *'These are not the Emperor's dogs'".*

In 1849, Norton sailed to San Francisco aboard the Dutch Schooner Franzika, enticed by reports that gold lay there simply for the taking. He carried a nest egg of $30,000 with which he opened a business selling supplies to gold miners. At the same time, he invested in land that was called San Francisco's Cow Hollow district.

Norton was considered one of San Francisco's most respected businessmen. He rebounded from the big fire of 1853 and diversified his operations. Already his friends were referring to him as *"Emperor"*. Norton was so successful that he was invited to become a member of the elite San Francisco Vigilance Committee.

Norton then conceived the bold idea of cornering the San Francisco rice market. The large Chinese population would provide a captive and hungry market for his rice. The only rice available was imported aboard cargo steamships.

Because of his previous investment successes, he soon signed on a number of ready investors. It was only a matter of days until he owned, practically speaking, all of the rice in San Francisco.

His downfall came when two ships arrived through the Golden Gate, both loaded with rice. While Norton had the money to buy one of the shipments, he could not afford to buy two such shipments. This meant he no longer held a corner on San Francisco's rice market.

With this glut of rice hitting the town, Norton was financially ruined. During the next three years, he spent most of his time in court, and emerged penniless in 1858.

Norton packed his meager belongings and disappeared from San Francisco for about nine months. There are no records of his whereabouts during the period he was gone.

Suddenly, in the late summer of 1859, Norton returned to San Francisco, walking proudly through the streets in a beaver hat and naval regalia. He was arguably mad, for soon after his return, he walked into the offices of the San Francisco Bulletin and presented them with this single sentence, which they ran in the next edition's front page:

"At the peremptory request of a large majority of the citizens of these United States, I, Joshua Norton, formerly of Algoa Bay, Cape of Good Hope, and now for the past nine years and ten months of San Francisco, California, declare and proclaim myself Emperor of these U.S., and in virtue of the authority thereby in me vested do hereby order and direct the representatives of the different States of the Union to assemble in Musical Hall of this city, on the 1st day of February next, then and there to make such alterations in the existing laws of the Union as may ameliorate the evils under which the country is laboring, and thereby cause confidence to exist, both at home and abroad, in our stability and integrity."

Norton I
Emperor of the United States
September 17, 1859

The populace loved him. When the people read his proclamation in the Bulletin, they began greeting him with deep bows and curtsies. In return, one writer said, "San Francisco has a wise and caring monarch to reign over its gilded cage."

The self-proclaimed emperor ruled his new domain by proclamation. It didn't faze him that not all of his edicts were carried out. If taxes or water rates were too high, he simply commanded that they be lowered. If there were inadequacies in city services, he ordered improvements.

He was also involved in national issues. On the eve of the Civil War, he temporarily dissolved the Union, and after the Prussian victory in 1872, he ordered a week of continuous celebration and thanksgiving.

Bay area newspapers were delighted and competed for the honor of printing his proclamations. Some accused newspapers of creating fake proclamations to stimulate reader interest, a practice against which the Emperor railed angrily.

Emperor Norton attended every public function or meeting, always arriving on foot or bicycle rather than coach, and performed daily rounds of his city's streets, making sure that police were on their beats and that cleanliness, harmony and order prevailed.

He was quick to anoint those that did good deeds. If he noticed someone performing a kind act, he might spontaneously ennoble him or her. The titles were especially popular with children, who would follow him in groups, looking everywhere for litter to pick up or old ladies to help across the street.

When Emperor Norton needed money, he simply issued his own script, such as the 50-cent bill above.

Norton's enchantment with San Francisco was returned in kind by San Francisco merchants and the public. His expenses were few. He could eat free at whatever restaurant suited his particular taste that day. He had three seats reserved for him at every theatrical performance (one for himself and one each for his famously well-behaved dogs, Bummer and Lazarus).

Author's note: There are some who say that Bummer and Lazarus were simply stray dogs and did not belong to Norton at all)

The city paid for Norton's majestic uniforms and the local Masonic Lodge paid for his small apartment. He paid the 50 cents a day lodging out of his receipts from begging.

If he needed cash, that was no problem. Norton simply printed his own currency. His cash was accepted without question. He didn't hesitate to levy imperial assessments on business owners. His normal procedure was to walk into the offices of an old business friend and politely announce an assessment of ten million or so dollars. The business owner could quickly talk him down to two or three, or perhaps a cigar, with which he would walk out completely satisfied.

San Francisco's police did not quite know how to handle the self-proclaimed emperor. In January of 1867, he was arrested by an over-zealous rookie policeman with the order that he "be confined for treatment of a mental disorder," and held at the police station pending a hearing.

The public was outraged. Every newspaper editorial denounced the action, and it was feared a riot would ensue. Police Chief Patrick Crowley himself opened the cell doors, and issued a lengthy public apology to the Emperor.

Norton was magnanimous about the whole affair and his relations with the police became much more congenial. He would lead their annual parades and inspect new cadets. These members of what he called his Imperial Constabulary saluted him when he passed.

There were some who believed Norton's madness was all an act, that one day he had decided to pull a prank, and because of the gullibility of the populace, got away with it for years.

17

Some felt that Emperor Norton's proclamations betrayed a complex, analytical man (though still mad). Samuel Clemens (Mark Twain), then a San Francisco newspaperman working next door to Norton's flophouse, saw Norton virtually every day.

Clemens hated those who belittled the self-styled emperor, especially newspaper columnist Arthur Evans, who wrote under the pseudonym of "Colonel Mustard".

Years later, Clemens revealed that he had based the character of the King in *Huckleberry Finn* on the eccentric Joshua Norton. In his book the *"Prince and the Pauper"*, a story of confused identities, Twain paid homage to Norton.

As emperor, Norton frequently sent cables to fellow rulers, offering surprisingly well informed advice. While many of the responses he got back were forgeries devised by his friends to make him happy, many were not.

King Kamehameha of Hawaii was so taken with the Emperor's insight and understanding that towards the end of his life he refused to recognize the U.S. State Department, saying instead he would deal only with representatives of the Empire.

Despite the fact that Norton was perceived to be mad, some of his proclamations became reality. For instance, he had issued numerous proclamations proposing and then finally commanding the construction of a suspension bridge linking San Francisco and Oakland.

He provided his own design sketches. His planned terminus is within a block of where the Bay

18

Bridge ends now. A plaque there is said to bear testimony of the emperor's foresight.

Norton I died quite suddenly of apoplexy on January 8, 1880, on the corner of California and Grant. He left no heirs. San Francisco mourned his passing. Ten thousand people, from all walks of life, lined up to view his remains. His funeral cortege was two miles long.

At 2:39 p.m. that day, during his funeral, San Francisco experienced a total eclipse of the sun. Fifty-four years later, Norton's coffin was reinterred at Woodlawn Cemetery in Colma. Flags throughout the city were lowered and businesses closed their doors. An estimated 60,000 people attended the ceremony, which was accompanied by full military honors.

Chapter 2

Splitting the State

One reason California is so large is the way it was divided into vast Mexican land grants. If the Mayflower had landed on California's Pacific coast, instead of the eastern seaboard, historians believe the state would have been cut up into several small states, similar to the New England region.

It takes longer to drive from California's northern border to its southern boundary than it does to travel the east coast from Maine, through six New England states, to Washington, D.C.

There have been at least 26 different proposals to split California since the time Alta (upper) California was poised to become a part of the United States.

During the Spanish period, the area that is now California was divided into two regions. There was "Baja (Lower) California and Alta (Upper) California, and it was called by the plural name *Las Californias*

The issue to divide California first arose when those in the southern part of the state wanted the Capital there. Those in the northern part of the state likewise wanted the government center.

The location of the Capital, it was believed, would dictate the area that would receive the greatest political considerations.

Visalia's Bill Maze pushed the idea to split California again. The former Assemblyman believes California should be split in half, creating a 51st state. The liberal coastal communities would be one state and the conservative central part of California would be another state.

The first attempts to split the state proposed locating California's Capital either in Monterey, Los Angeles, or in San Diego.

The division issue carried over into the State Constitutional Convention in 1849, and there have been perennial proposals that California be split into two or more parts since.

Because of California's size, there are major differences among the regions.

22

Residents in the eastern region, that contains desert and mountains, felt they were short-changed by politicians who favored the coastal section of the state.

The southern part of California developed more slowly than did the northern section. This led to harsh complaints from southerners that they were being unfairly taxed and were not sufficiently represented in the legislature.

Northern California grew rapidly, fueled by the gold rush, but thrived also on an economy that included farming, lumber, and recreation.

The population and the political power of California shifted from northern California to the south in the 1960s. This led to a host of complaints from the north.

Northerners felt they were being overtaxed to pay for Southern California's education, social programs, and justice system.

Water was another divisive issue between the north and the south. The south was dependent on the north for its water. Northerners felt that the dams and facilities necessary to transport water to the south were causing unwanted geographic and climatic changes.

Some maintained that the earthquakes, such as one in Oroville in 1975, were a result of the construction of water facilities.

Advocates of dividing the state voiced a common grievance: California was just too big, and, therefore ungovernable.

Proposals to divide the state first appeared in 1849, during the state's first Constitutional Convention in Monterey. In 1993, the *California Historian* listed 26 separate proposals to break up California

In 1864, a state-splitting measure was placed on the ballot, approved by voters, signed by the Governor, and sent to Congress. Congress did not approve it.

Some upstart communities, such as the town of Rough and Ready, facetiously holds a one-day "secession" party each year in which it advocates becoming an independent "republic".

No state in the U.S. has been split into two or more regions since 1862, when the western part of the state of Virginia opposed Virginia's secession from the Union in 1861, and Congress recognized it as the state of West Virginia.

Most proposals to divide California would split the state horizontally into two parts, either at the Tehachapi Mountains or at a northern point just above or below Sacramento. There was at least one suggestion, however, that the state be divided vertically into East and West California.

Another suggestion proposed dividing California into three states, North, South, and Central California. This proposal recognizes the central part of the state (*the valley*) as having separate needs from the more urban northern and southern regions.

Still another proposal would divide California into a number of small states. This suggestion is deemed to be a tongue-in-cheek suggestion that would

Balkanize California into small states lacking adequate resources and virtually no power nationally.

Perhaps the most radical suggestion, and also done facetiously, would make California a separate nation. This proposal was the brainchild of San Jose Mercury newsman Ted Bredt, who noted that California's resources and financial potential are larger than those of many nations.

In 1849, Jose Antonio Carrillo, a southern delegate to the Constitutional Convention, proposed a split of California at San Luis Obispo. The southern part of the state would become a territory, while the northern part would become a state.

Other delegates at the Constitutional Convention proposed including what is now California, but also Nevada, Utah, and Arizona in the new state. This proposal was rejected out of hand as it would create a state so large it could not be fairly represented in the legislature, and its laws could not be efficiently and effectively administered.

During the first ten years following the first constitutional convention, the legislature received annual proposals of how to divide California into more than one state.

One Southern California group would form a state in the area south of Monterey, which they would call Central California.

In 1852, some Californians near the Oregon border expressed their strong dissatisfaction over high taxes, poor mail service, and the lack of military protection against California Indian tribes. They wanted to form the State of Shasta.

There were attempts by one northern California area to separate from California altogether. This was in 1856, when Isaac Newton Roop, the founder of Susanville, and Peter Lassen, the explorer for whom Lassen County was named, sought to form an independent territory.

This territory would be made up by parts of both northern California and of Nevada, which they would call Nataqua, a word, meaning woman, in the local Indian language.

Later, in 1854, resolutions were drafted to form the State of Klamath, which would include portions of Northern California and of Southern Oregon. The proponents claimed the area encompassed in their proposal was distinctly different from either the rest of California or of Oregon. This was a popular proposal, but was eventually defeated because of problems with Indians in the area.

Also in 1854, San Bernardino Assemblyman Jefferson Hunt introduced a bill for the creation of a new state of Columbia, covering the area from Santa Cruz to the Mexican Border.

It is unlikely that California will ever be divided. Any proposal aimed at splitting the state must gain the consent of the legislature, and then be approved by Congress as well. Still, the state-splitting issue is likely to emerge many times in the future, as it is an easy way for a politician to get space in the press.

Chapter 3

William Ide was president for one day.

The President of California

The Republic of California lasted only 24 days, but during that time, a president was named and a proclamation issued proclaiming its independence.

The Republic of California was the result of a citizen uprising to protest the possibility of the province being ceded to the British Empire by Mexican authorities, which were in power at the time.

Settlers believed that the *Californios*, the Mexican population of California, were stirring up the Indians to attack unprotected farms and ranches. They thought a force of Mexicans would soon attempt to drive all Americans from the Valley.

U.S. Army Captain John C. Fremont initiated some of this distrust by provoking Mexican authorities and stirring up the American settlers by spreading rumors of Mexican actions against the settlers.

The number of American settlers on the Pacific Coast in the 1840s was small, but steadily increasing. In 1841, there were only 30 such settlers. By 1845, the number had increased to 250.

In June 1846, the Americans were told that a Mexican military, led by General Jose Castro, was on its way to the Sacramento Valley, destroying crops, burning houses and driving off the cattle of settlers.

Although untrue, the rumor, along with the presence of Fremont and his troops, was enough to spur the Americans into action. A half-a-dozen settlers, led by the raw-boned illiterate frontiersman Ezekiel Merritt, seized a band of horses designed for the use of the Mexican General

Castro and the settlers decided to revolt against the Mexican government.

The Original California Bear Flag.

This confrontation led to what is known in history as "The Bear Flag Revolt".

Led by Merritt and William B. Ide, the American settlers occupied the town of Sonoma, taking its leading inhabitants prisoner, including the influential Don Mariano Guadalupe Vallejo, even though he was an advocate of California's annexation to the United States.

The settlers proclaimed the creation of the Republic of California. Ide was declared president of the new republic. The settlers issued a statement justifying their action, and adopted the so-called Bear Flag as the new standard of the commonwealth.

Their flag was hastily put together from a piece of unbleached cotton cloth, snipped from the petticoat of a boardinghouse keeper. The flag measured five feet long by three feet wide.

The design consisted of the crude figure of a grizzly bear, a five-pointed star, roughly outlined in ink, and a strip of red flannel, sewn across the lower edge of the cotton cloth.

Underneath the star and the grizzly bear design was printed in bold red capitals, the words, "California Republic".

Mariano Vallejo signed some articles of surrender and then entertained his captors with his best wine and brandy.

The group of settlers now seemed to accept Ide as their leader. The Bear Flaggers raised their standard over the plaza at Sonoma and declared the pueblo as their headquarters. Not a shot had been fired nor a life lost.

The American settlers determined they could not count on support from Fremont. Some suggested abandoning the town and retreating. William B. Ide stepped forth and made a rousing speech, declaring that he would die before retreating in disgrace.

The entire affair was confusing to the Mexican Californios, who were not aware of any aggression. There was no war between Mexico and the United States that anyone in *California* knew about, but the Americans were intent on establishing some position of legality.

The Americans set up headquarters at Sonoma, and had an official flag, but were unsure what they should do next.

Before the Americans and the Mexicans engaged in any serious struggles, another event happened that solved the bewilderment of the Bear Flaggers.

Commodore John D. Sloat, commander of the United States Pacific Squadron, had official orders to seize California if he should learn of a war between California and Mexico. Sloat soon learned of events in the northern part of California, including the Bear Flag Revolt.

Sloat was nervous about his position, because the British Fleet had been dogging him off the coast of California. This heightened his fears that the British might come in and take California first.

On the morning of July 7, 1846, Sloat landed two hundred and fifty marines and sailors at Monterey. They marched to the Customs House, read Sloat's proclamation of protection for California, and raised the United States flag.

Another officer was dispatched to Sonoma to raise the American flag there, replacing the Bear Flag, which had been flying since mid-June.

This action brought the Bear Flag Revolt to an abrupt end, and a hasty conclusion to William B. Ide's position as California's first and only president.

Chapter 4

Women First to Find Gold

Three women may have been first to discover gold in California. Their discovery is dated a full year before James Marshall discovered gold at Sutter's Mill in Coloma, a discovery that attracted hordes of gold seekers to California.

The women were Mrs. Adna Hecox, Mrs. Joseph Aram, and Mrs. Isaac Isbell. They were part of a wagon train coming to California from the mid-west.

It was while doing laundry in a tributary stream of the Yuba River that the women noticed the glittering flakes clinging to their towels and sheets. Mrs. Hecox, who tells of the experience in her book, *"California Caravan"*, said she gathered several of the shiny specks of glitter into her apron. When she showed them to her minister husband, he guffawed, telling her she was foolhardy. In a fit of woman's temper, Mrs. Hecox tossed her flakes to the wind.

Mrs. Aram, doing her laundry further downstream shouted to the other women to hurry over. "I do believe I have found gold," she declared. She held up a nugget the size of a dime. She tucked the nugget away until the wagon train arrived at Sutter's Fort in Sacramento.

There, the nugget was assayed, and was indeed pure gold.

The men in the wagon train marked the site of Mrs. Aram's find, hoping to one-day return. None ever came back.

"This country was in such a tumult at the time," wrote Mrs. Hecox. "People had little opportunity to search for gold until their affairs were in a more settled condition and the people were out of danger." Had the women's discovery of gold in the Yuba River tributary in 1846 been heralded as loudly as that of James Marshall a year later at Coloma, history might indeed have been written differently.

Chapter 5

Wheelbarrow Johnny

Instead of seeking gold on arriving in California, John Studebaker took a job making wheelbarrows in a blacksmith shop.

Nineteen-year-old John Studebaker came west to search for gold. Instead, he made wheelbarrows.

When the young Studebaker arrived at Old Dry Diggings (now Placerville), it was the last day of

August 1853. Placerville, at the time, was one of the more important towns in California, and was bidding to be the state's capital, in competition with Sacramento, San Francisco, and Chinese Camp.

Placerville was well known throughout the nation during the gold rush, and was far ahead of some of the other towns such as Poker Flat, Red Dog, You Bet, Whiskey Town, and Petticoat Slide, Rough and Ready, Skunk Gulch, and Angel's Camp.

For one thing, Placerville was strategically located on the main transcontinental trail.

John Studebaker arrived in Placerville driving a wagon he built in his father's wagon shop back home in South Bend, Indiana. John's father had five sons who built wagons. They settled on a design which became world famous. It was the Conestoga wagon.

Young John's bankroll consisted of a pitiful fifty cents when he arrived in Placerville. He lost his original bankroll of $68 to a card shark during a stopover in Council Bluffs, Iowa.

As the wagon train arrived at Placerville, local citizens quickly gathered around. One man asked aloud, "Is there a wagon maker among you?" Several men in the wagon train pointed to young Studebaker and the wagon he had built for the trip west.

"My name is H.L. Hinds," the man said. "I'm the blacksmith and I have a good job for a man who wants work. Want the job?" he asked Studebaker.

Young John hesitated. "I came to California to dig gold," he said. Hinds walked away.

Thomas Edison in 1902 Studebaker electric car.

It was then a man who overheard the conversation said to Studebaker. "I don't know you from Adam, but I can't help giving you a piece of advice. Take that job and take it quick. You'll have plenty of time to look for gold. There are hundreds of disappointed gold seekers for every one who strikes pay dirt. They haven't a penny. Some of them are hungry. You're lucky to be offered a job five minutes after you get here. Grab it, boy."

To John, the directness of the advice was compelling. He hurried after the disappearing Hinds and told him he had reconsidered and would like the job after all. He later learned the gentleman who gave him the advice was Dr. Wortham, the best physician in town.

The work at the blacksmith shop consisted of repairing miners' picks and pans as well as considerable stagecoach repairing. The big demand, however, was for wheelbarrows.

"Can you make a wheelbarrow," Hinds asked.

"I sure can," replied John. "That is, I can try."

John's first wheelbarrow was a dismal failure. It was rickety, clumsy, and made of green pitch pine. It had taken him two days to build it. When he finished, his employer laughed, and said, "That's a hell of a wheelbarrow. Try again."

John's second attempt produced a much better product. By the time he had produced a third one, he found the knack of producing a sturdy and rugged wheelbarrow. He soon was given the name, "Wheelbarrow Johnny."

By 1855, John sold his wheelbarrows for $10 each and saved $3,000. To fulfill his original desire to be a gold miner, he staked a claim. It was not profitable, but he was able to glean a few pieces of gold to show his family in Indiana. By continuing to work at making wheelbarrows, by the fall of 1857 Studebaker's savings increased to $7,000.

At this time, John received a letter from his 26-year-old brother Clem, who was making wagons with his brother Henry in South Bend. Clem wrote that their H. & C. Studebaker Company, could only turn out a dozen wagons a year because the brothers did all the work themselves. They could not buy supplies in large lots because of a lack of money.

Clem told John that while they were doing all right, they could do so much more if they had the capital. Instead of only building a dozen wagons a year, Clem envisioned building 100 or even 200 wagons each year. A sound thinker, John knew that South Bend was the perfect town in which to build wagons.

Studebaker made a decision. He would work right there in Hangtown until the next spring, saving all the money he could. He would then return to South Bend with $8,000 in his pocket. This he would put into H. & C. Studebaker.

In 1856, a fire started in a small Placerville restaurant on Sacramento Street. It spread to neighboring buildings, turning Hangtown into a roaring inferno.

John Studebaker was a member of the volunteer fire brigade. He was directed to fight a fire on a nearby street, while blacksmith Joseph Hinds stayed behind to protect the shop.

Once the fire jumped Sacramento Street, it soon reached the blacksmith shop, burning it to the ground.

When the fire was brought under control, John returned to the shop and he and Hinds dug up the floorboards where a few jars of gold coins were stashed. Happily, the intense heat had not damaged the cache.

Sadly, however, young Studebaker could never identify the places where he had buried another part of the horde. After some digging, he did unearth about $8,000. He discontinued his search so the blacksmith could reopen his shop.

During a stopover in New York on his way back to South Bend, John saw carriages in Central Park. He made a mental note that while the West would need heavy-duty wagons, light buggies might also be needed in Council Bluffs, Sioux City, Denver, or Sacramento.

H. & C. Studebaker did a thriving business during the Civil War, supplying the Union Army with a steady supply of wagons. The reliability and ruggedness of the Studebaker wagons became legendary, and the Studebaker Corporation made its place in history.

Studebaker Brothers Manufacturing Company was organized in 1868. By 1875, it was the largest builder of wagons in the world, with over one million dollars in sales.

The Studebaker Corporation produced an electric horseless carriage in 1902, followed by the manufacture of a gasoline-powered automobile in 1904. At the head of the corporation was J. M. Studebaker, formerly known as *"Wheelbarrow Johnny"*.

Back in Hangtown, the community still holds its annual John M. Studebaker World Championship Wheelbarrow Races. Contestants race their wheelbarrows down the track at El Dorado County Fairgrounds in an attempt to reach the "ore pile", and then navigate a series of obstacles.

They begin the race by pushing their wheelbarrows to the ore pile, where they must use a gold pan to fill a gunnysack with what they estimate is 50 pounds of sand and gravel. From there, they scurry to cross a fallen tree and a dry creek bed with their wheelbarrows in tow. The grand finale is to go over Joe's Hill and cross the Water Hole.

The object is to get to the top of the hill as quickly as they can, and once at the peak, go straight down the other side and into the water hole. They must float, swim or otherwise get their wheelbarrow through the water and mud and on to the finish line.

Contestants must still have 50 pounds of "ore" in their bag at the finish. It isn't uncommon for a person coming in fourth or fifth place to win the race when the frontrunners come up short at the weigh-in.

Wheelbarrow Johnny would surely have endorsed the event.

Chapter 6

Japanese Settle Gold Hill

The gravesite of Okei, the young Japanese girl that helped settle Gold Hill.

Three Japanese families arrived at Gold Hill in El Dorado County on June 8, 1869. There they founded the Wakamatsu Tea and Silk Colony. Their contingent was small, but significant, as they were among the first Japanese to immigrate to California.

The *Alta Daily News* in San Francisco devoted considerable space to the fact that the Japanese arrivals landed in San Francisco, bringing with them 50,000 three-year-old *kuwa* trees, which are used in the production of silk.

The blossom of a tea plant

In addition, the Japanese brought great numbers of all kinds of bamboo.

The Japanese traveled aboard the Pacific Mail Steamship Company, which began passenger and mail service from California to Japan and China in 1867. This is the same line that later carried many Chinese laborers to California.

The Japanese colony expected 500 three-year-old saplings of the wax tree and six million tea seeds to arrive at their Wakamatsu Tea and Silk Farm in later shipments. The tale of the Wakamatsu

Colony is told in a paper written by John Van Sant, who later moved to Japan and wrote regular newspaper pieces. He wrote the paper to as a thesis for a history course.

Matsudaira Katamori was among the immigrants that arrived at Gold Hill in 1869. In Japan, he was a respected lord of the Aizu domain in northern Japan. He became a prominent participant in the bloody and bitter Boshin War. Unfortunately, he fought on the losing side. Despite his prominent role in the war, he was spared the death sentence by the victors.

During the turmoil in Japan, Matsudaira became associated with a German named John Henry Schnell, a merchant and gunrunner from whom Matsudaira had purchased arms.

Matsudaira let Schnell persuade him to travel to California where word spread that gold was found in the tiny northern California town of Coloma.

Schnell, married to a Japanese woman. He was considered *persona non grata* in Japan for selling arms to the losers. Soon after the end of the Boshin War, Schnell suggested to Matsudaira that land could be easily purchased for farming in California.

Schnell needed Matsudaira's financial support for the California venture. After arriving in San Francisco, the group, which included Schnell, his wife, and six Japanese colonists, departed for Sacramento by boat. From Sacramento, they traveled to Placerville by hired wagons, arriving in June 1869.

Schnell immediately purchased 160 acres of land and a house in Gold Hill for $5,000 from Charles Graner, a San Francisco businessman who owned substantial tracts of land in El Dorado County.

Gold Hill lay between Hangtown (now Placerville) and the town of Coloma where James Marshall discovered gold.

The Wakamatsu Tea and Silk Farm prospered in the beginning. The *San Francisco Call* reported on the products of the Japanese Colony being exhibited by Schnell at the Horticultural Fair in San Francisco:

"Herr Schnell of the Japanese Colony in Gold Hill, El Dorado County," the paper noted, "makes a fine display of Japanese plants, grown from imported shrubs and seeds. Amongst his articles are fine healthy tea plants, which were planted on March 14, 1870 last. These plants are about four inches high and are vigorous and healthy. He also exhibited samples of rice plants and a specimen of the Japanese pepper tree."

The initial success of the Wakamatsu Tea and Silk Farm soon faded. Its demise came from two common causes of failure on California's frontier, the lack of water and the lack of money.

Not only was California suffering from a drought during the late 1860s and early 1870s, but what water there was dried up because gold miners damned up a nearby creek.

Without water, the colony was unable to produce tea, silk, or any other products for market. Because of this, and his own financial mismanagement,

Schnell ran out of money. Schnell took his wife and children and left the colony in May 1871. He never returned.

Before leaving, he surreptitiously sold the Wakamatsu Colony's 160 acres of land to the El Dorado County government.

The colony broke up and the Japanese inhabitants scattered to nearby areas of California. A few returned to Japan.

The fates of three of the Wakamatsu Colonists are known. Masumizu Kuninosuke was a 20-year old carpenter that arrived at Gold Hill with the second group of immigrants coming to the area from Japan. After the breakup of the colony, he went to Sacramento and married. His bride was the daughter of a Blackfoot Indian and her husband, a freed slave.

Masumizu, who was called "Kuni", became a fisherman and farmer. He owned his own fish shop on Second Street. He also worked part time as an interpreter in Sacramento Courts because he could speak Japanese, English, and Spanish. He died at the age of 66 in 1915, and is buried in Colusa.

Sakurai Matsunosuke and a young girl named Okei went to live with the Francis Veerkamp family. Veerkamp managed the property where the colony was located before the Japanese arrived. He was able to acquire the property back from El Dorado County.

Okei, worked as a nursemaid for Mrs. Veerkamp's two children. She died of illness at the age of 19. She was buried at Gold Hill. A monument marks Okei's grave, which is near a monument dedicated by then California Governor Ronald Reagan, observing the location of the Wakamatsu Tea and Silk Farm. . Descendents of the Veerkamps live in the foothills of the Sierras.

Chapter 7

Black Man Makes His Mark

A painting of Jim Beckwourth by John M. Thompson.

James Beckwourth was born in Fredericksburg, Virginia, on April 6, 1798. Jim was born into slavery (1798-1866.) He came to California with his father and was freed.

He was the son of a black slave woman and a white Revolutionary War army officer.

His father was a Missouri planter. Young Jim's courage and daring on the frontier soon earned him the title "the famous mulatto of the plains". He was a member of an elite fur-trapping clique and traveled with the great mountain men of the time, Jedediah Smith, Louis Vasquez and Jim Bridger.

During his trapping days, Beckwourth lived with the Crow Indians and became a chief. When the fur business waned in the 1840s, Beckwourth moved to New Mexico to trade. He married a señorita.

While his deeds and adventures easily matched those of Kit Carson, Jim Bridger, Davy Crockett and Daniel Boone, his story was nearly lost to history. One writer said, "Probably no man ever lived who had met with more personal adventure involving danger to life".

Beckwourth was wise in the ways of Indians and learned to speak their language. He was a crack shot with a rifle and was said to never waste a bullet. He was adept with a bowie knife and a tomahawk.

After living with the Indians for several years, Beckwourth became bored with his life among the Crow and Blackfoot tribes. In 1837, he became chief scout for General John C. Fremont.

Later, while wandering and prospecting in the Pit River Country of northern California, Beckwourth saw a distinct difference in the elevation of the mountains in the distance. There was one spot in the formation that appeared much lower than any others.

The following spring, he led a prospecting party of twelve men, heading in the direction of the gap in the mountains. The group entered upon an extensive valley at the northwest extremity of the Sierra range.

The verdant valley was colored by many varieties of wildflowers. There were chattering magpies as well as handsome plumaged birds. Wild geese and ducks were swimming on the surface of a cool crystal stream.

Herds of deer and antelope were abundant. Their boldness indicated to Beckwourth that they had never heard the shot of a rifle. He became convinced that he and his party were probably the first men to set foot in the area.

The group crossed the valley and reached the waters of the Yuba. Further on, they came to the waters of the *"Truchy"* (Beckwourth's obvious misspelling of the Truckee River).

He noticed the *"Truchy"* was flowing in an eastward direction, convincing him that he and his party were on the eastern slope of the Sierra mountain range. He was soon convinced that this might be the best route for a wagon road over the Sierras.

Back in Marysville, he convinced the mayor and other citizens that this route could be a boon for the town. The wagon route would make Marysville the principal starting place for emigrants who would otherwise go to Sacramento.

Marysville's mayor assured Beckwourth that he would be handsomely rewarded if he could develop such a route. The reward, he suggested, might be as much as six thousand to ten thousand dollars.

When Beckwourth guided the first wagons down a ridge into Marysville, the citizens began a wild celebration. The event became so wild in its frenzy that part of the town burned to the ground.

It was a devastating event for Beckwourth, for with the fire went his hopes of a monetary reward. The mayor, while congratulating Beckwourth on his feat in opening the pass, informed the trailblazer that the fire made it beyond his power to pay him any money.

With the exception of two hundred dollars subscribed by some liberal-minded citizens of Marysville, Beckwourth's only reward was the naming of the trail in his honor. "The Beckwourth Trail" still exists, beginning just a few miles from Reno, Nevada.

The trail he discovered was later used by thousands of pioneers and gold seekers on their way to California. The trail was a lower pass over the mountains that proved to be far safer for emigrants than the Donner Trail.

Even with his disappointment over not receiving the money he was promised, Beckwourth loved the area through which his trail traversed. He established his War Horse Ranch in the upper Feather River Valley, where he built a hotel and trading post.

His was the first stop for emigrants using the trail on their way to the gold fields. It became a prosperous operation for Beckwourth, but created tension among other settlers. They did not like seeing a black man being more successful than themselves.

Instead of facing more racial resentment, Beckwourth returned to Denver, where he died in 1866.

Legend has it that the Crow Indians honored him at a farewell feast to urge him to stay with them and lead them to greatness again. He refused and it is said the Crows poisoned him to keep his body and powerful spirit within their land.

Chapter 8

The Pit River

The Pit River

Few rivers in the west have a more controversial name than the Pit River. There are some who say the stream is not entitled to a name at all as it is really just an extension of the Sacramento River and should thus be called the "Upper Sacramento".

The Pit River got its name from trappers of the Hudson Bay Company, who wandered around the area in search of good pelts. The trappers were amazed by the many "blind" holes dug by local Indians to catch wild animals. They understandably dubbed the river the "Pit River".

The holes, or pits, dug by the Indians were located in places where their enemies and wild game were likely to pass. The pits, according to Joaquin

Miller, in his book, *"Life Amongst the Modocs"*, were dangerous traps, ten or fifteen feet deep. They were small at the mouth, but made to diverge in descent much like a jug.

It was impossible for any man or beast that fell in one of the traps to escape. Making the traps even more formidable, the Indians set the antlers of deer and elk in the bottom of the pit to pierce whoever or whatever fell into the traps.

Indian women dug the pits, using only sticks and baskets. They carried the earth from the holes and threw it in the river,. These holes were a great nuisance to settlers.

While "Pit River" was recognized as the correct spelling for the stream, and appeared on Hood's Map as such in 1838, it was called the "Pitt River". In 1841, one cartographer, in an obvious ploy to curry favor with the English Statesman, Pitt, called it Pitt's River. The same cartographer changed the name of Goose Lake to Pitt's Lake.

In 1850, a Lieutenant Williamson surveyed the area and changed the name back to "Pit", and went on to justify the spelling by stating, "We passed many pits about six feet deep and lightly covered with twigs and grass. The river derives its name from these pits, which are dug by the Indians to entrap game."

Even with Williamson's explanation, many of the newspapers continued to use the 'Pitt River" name in their news stories.

Josiah D. Whitney, director of the State Geological Survey from 1860 to 1874 (Mt. Whitney was named after him), substantiated the fact that the Pit River was an extension of the Sacramento.

Others, including Ferdinand von Leicht and J.D. Hoffman, who mapped the area, hedged on the subject of what the river should be called. They simply called the stream "the Upper Sacramento or Pit River".

Finally, in 1901, the Geological Survey issued the Redding atlas sheet and officially labeled the river "the Pit River". It has remained the Pit River ever since.

Chapter 9

The Final Chapter on Ishi

Ishi with a bow and arrow.

Ishi was the last survivor of the Yahi tribe. Ishi wandered into the town of Oroville in 1911, long after it was believed the tribe died out. He seemed dazed, naked, and starving. He appeared to be in his 40s.

The Yahi's were living a furtive existence near Mount Lassen. Settlers in the area didn't know there were any of the Yahi's tribe left.

The little Indian achieved almost immediate fame and became the subject of intensive study by anthropologists. When he died in 1916, his body was cremated and his ashes buried at Colma, south of

San Francisco. However, neither his body nor his spirit was complete, according to Butte County Indians.

His brain, according to records of the anthropologists who studied and befriended him, had been preserved. But no one seemed to know where the organ was kept. The brain was preserved against the express wishes Ishi made while still alive.

A University of California, San Francisco, historian, and a Duke University anthropologist began the search for Ishi's brain after they read the organ was preserved.

Indians in Butte County wanted to find the remains so that Ishi could be reburied in the wilderness area named for him in Lassen Volcanic National Park. They believed the burial would be useless unless all of the remains were reunited.

"It is very important that he be returned here as a complete person, a complete spirit," Arthur Angle, director of the Butte County Native American Cultural Committee, told the Los Angeles Times.

The search for Ishi's brain reads much like a detective novel.

A Los Angeles Times article sent Nancy Rockafellar (sic), a historian at UC-San Francisco, on a search to see if the brain was at her university. She interviewed elderly physicians and searched medical records.

She expanded her search to records at the Bancroft Library at UC-Berkeley, where the papers of anthropologist Arthur Kroeber were stored.

Kroeber was one of the anthropologists who brought Ishi to University of California for further study.

Ishi discussing his life with an audience.

Finally, Nancy Rockafellar learned that the brain might was sent to the Smithsonian Institution. Smithsonian officials dismissed this as rumor, and Rockafellar said, "I just hit a brick wall."

Rockafellar then joined forces with Duke University anthropologist Orin Starn, who was in the process of writing a book about Ishi, and who was also interested in locating the brain.

Starn stumbled on some firmer information by going to the Bancroft Library and searching under "Smithsonian". There he found correspondence between Kroeber and Ales Hrdlicka (sic) (who in 1916 was Smithsonian's curator of physical anthropology.

Hrdlicka, he learned, collected about 300 human brains, studying whether there was a correlation between brain weight and body weight in humans.

Kroeber became distraught on Oct. 27, 1916, when Ishi died, and furious when he learned that the Indian's body had been autopsied against his wishes.

He wrote to Hrdlicka. *"Dear Dr. Hrdlicka: I find that at Ishi's death last spring, his brain was removed and preserved. There is none here who can put it to scientific use. If you wish it, I shall be glad to deposit it in the National Museum collection."*

Hrdlicka replied: *My Dear Dr. Kroeber: I hardly need to say that we shall be very glad to receive and to take care of Ishi's brain, and if a suitable opportunity occurs to have it suitably worked up."*

The brain was sent on January 15, 1917. At some point, it was transferred to a warehouse in Suitland, Maryland, where it languished for decades in preservatives in a tank.

It wasn't until January 1999, that Starn was able to confirm the whereabouts of Ishi's brain.

Ishi's history captures the imagination. The land where the Yahi tribe of California Indians existed was a region of endless ridges and cliff-walled canyons. The Yahi tribe frequented the very wild area along Mill and Deer creeks, east of the Sacramento River in the very northern region of California.

Except during times when heavy snows and turbulent weather brought them to the verge of starvation, the Yahi moved about their small hillside community, safe from intrusion by the white man.

The Yahi was one of four dialectic divisions of the Yana tribe. It comprised only 300 to 400 souls at its utmost. These Indians suffered heavily at the hands of white men, but were also subjected to frequent attacks by other Indian tribes. The Yahi were never even partially sheltered by reservations. They survived strictly by their wiles and their instincts.

The region where the Yahi lived contained patches in which the brush was almost impenetrable. There were many caves in the faces of the cliffs, providing the diminishing tribe with hundreds of places to hide from their real or supposed enemies.

The small tribe might not have survived as long as it did except for the fact the area had few minerals, no marketable lumber, and no rich bottom lands to attract the California newcomers.

The Yahi settled into the region, giving them a retreat from which they could conveniently raid other regions, but at the same time provided them with a position virtually impenetrable by their enemies. Only a concerted plan by outsiders could ever rout them.

Enemy action inevitably came around 1865. It occurred after numerous skirmishes with small parties of Americans. In one disastrous fight, more often labeled as a slaughter, a large contingent of the Yahi Indians was surrounded and literally exterminated in an early-morning attack by a group of settlers.

For years the tribe was believed extinct. There were infrequent reports that a cattleman or a hunter had spotted "wild and naked Indians" who fled like deer. Other reports noted that deserted cabins in the hills had been rifled. Settlers in and around the Mill Creek area generally scoffed at these stories.

When the white invasion of California began, the Yahi escaped the fate of other Indian tribes, who tended to become hangers-on of the coming civilization. The Yahis followed their own time-honored rule and took refuge in their foothill retreats, remaining a so-called "wild" tribe.

But the white men settling the area refused to leave these Indians alone. If a sheep was eaten by a mountain lion, it was blamed on the Indians. If provisions in a remote cattle camp turned up missing, it was sure to be the sneaky work of the Indians. Murders committed in out-of-the-way places were attributed to the Indians.

According to the "Handbook of Indians of California," the last printed reference to the Yahi is that of Stephen Powers, an anthropologist who knew them by their Maidu name of Kombo.

Powers told of how a couple of hunters encountered two men, two women, and a child, but the Indians soon escaped into the brush. They were considered the last survivors of the Yahi group.

In 1908, a party of surveyors worked half way up the side of Deer Creek Canyon. They ran their line almost into a hidden camp in which four middle-aged and elderly Indians were living. The four fled to the brushy hillsides.

In the camp, surveyors found arrows, implements, baskets, stored food and some American objects, which obviously had been stolen. What was clearer is that for 43 years, this tiny Indian household had remained unknown; it was a remnant of what was once a nation.

The remnant group sustained itself by hiding in sheltered spots, smothering their camp smoke, and crawling under brush so as to leave no trail. Their ingenuity at eluding their white pursuers showed a marvelous instinct.

It was at this point, in 1911, that Ishi, the single survivor of the Yahi, stumbled into Oroville. He was alone, weaponless, and, pressed by hunger.

The fact that he was considered the last wild Indian in the United States drew wide interest. There was little question of the genuineness of his aboriginal condition. He was practically naked, in obvious terror, and knew no English.

Ishi told one group that he was the Indian doctor for the Yahi group. The Yahi Indian doctors, when they lost patients, would burn their hair off because their hair was supposed to be the evil spirit.

Then if they lost another patient, the doctor was put to death. So Ishi's last patient was his mother. He knew that the few Indians left would kill him. That's why he ran away. That's why he went towards the Oroville area.

His name, Ishi, is an anglicized translation meaning man. Ishi was placed into the hands of T.T.

Waterman, an anthropologist at the University of California, who had traveled to Oroville to pick up his charge.

The trip back to San Francisco entailed taking a train. As the train neared, Ishi only wanted to hide behind something. He had seen such trains before, but only in the distance, and did not realize they ran on tracks. He always laid down in the grass or hid behind a bush or tree until the train monsters were out of sight.

This last member of the Yahi tribe learned to speak English slowly and brokenly, and would converse on all topics in his own tongue, with the exception of the fate of his kinsmen. On this subject, he was silent. Ishi never learned to shake hands.

Ishi's life ended in1916, when he was about 50 or 55 years old, due to a bout with tuberculosis to which he had never developed immunity.

Chapter 10

Capitol Comes to Rest

The first State Capital of California was in San Jose;
here the legislatures of the new State pose for a
photograph.

California had a difficult time selecting a site for
the state's capital. A variety of state capital sites
were looked at before a permanent one was chosen.

The first legislative session met in Monterey, the
second in San Jose, and the third in Vallejo. Each of
these towns offered uncomfortable and inadequate
facilities.

When Californians adopted a constitution in 1849, it did so without the federal government's consent and without a site for a permanent capitol building. The lack of a definite capital site was the subject of legislative rancor and squabbling for years.

To clarify for readers, "capital" and "capitol" are pronounced alike but often confused. Webster defines "capital" as the city serving the location of government, while "capitol" is the building in which legislators meet.

There was a scramble by various California towns to get the capital located in their community. San Jose citizens lobbied hard while other legislators wanted Monterey as the state capital site.

Legislators first came up with a compromise. The first session, they decided, would be held in Monterey because this city already had a building. Subsequent sessions would be held in San Jose.

The first California Capitol was therefore Colton Hall in Monterey, where the constitutional convention had first met. The building measured 30 feet by 70 feet, and its upper story had served just fine for delegates to California's first Constitution Convention. Colton Hall was built as a combination town hall and schoolhouse.

Representatives from San Jose emphasized that their city was the true center of California and the capital should be there. Further, wealthy citizens had donated land for the proposed capitol grounds.

Erected in 1852, this historic building was ostensibly intended for Benicia City Hall, offered as the state capitol and promptly accepted, it had that honor from February 4, 1853 to February 25, 1854. Deeded to the state in 1951, it was one of the four locations of the capitol building.

There were other proposals. One was to put the Capitol in the beautiful Mission San Luis Obispo. Another, locate it at San Francisco, as it could provide commercial possibilities. The delegate making this proposal, however, assured the legislators there would be no free land offered for a capitol-building site.

Another suggestion was to locate the California capital at Stockton, while another said Santa

68

Barbara would be the ideal site because of its climate and location.

State Capital at Vallejo

One reason for moving the capital from Monterey was the contention that Americans wanted change. They did want to follow Hispanic customs.

California's first legislators did not run for election with the thought of making a lot of money. The first salaries were set at $16 per Diem, with $16 for each twenty miles traveled to and from the Capital. The salaries reflected the high cost of stagecoach travel between San Jose and San Francisco. Fares were paid by a pinch of gold dust, generally considered as an ounce, which was valued at $16.

The first legislature was dissatisfied with the routes and facilities to and from San Jose. They therefore brought forward new capital site proposals.

The next proposal to win approval was to locate the capitol building at Vallejo.

Proponents argued that nine-tenths of the state's officials traveled through Vallejo on the way to San Jose. Moving the capitol building there would save thousands of dollars in money paid out for mileage.

Mariana Vallejo deeded an indefinite number of acres for the proposed capital city. Five commissioners were named to determine the actual site. The commissioners reported back that if projected plans were followed, Vallejo would be a city envied and copied worldwide.

While it appeared California had found a permanent capital site, uproar occurred when disgruntled merchants and residents of San Jose charged that bribery had taken place in locating the new capital in Vallejo.

Despite the promises of grandiose facilities for the legislators in Vallejo, work proceeded slowly because of expensive and hard to obtain materials. A stream of events caused consternation among the legislators arriving for the legislative session at Vallejo.

The boat from San Francisco grounded some fifty feet before reaching the wharf and passengers had to be rowed ashore. The streets of Vallejo were filled with tar-like mud, and the legislators found it difficult to walk to the stark frame building that was to be the state's new capitol.

There was scant seating in the building for the legislators. Boards were stretched across nail kegs to form benches, some of which broke under the weight of those seated.

Lodging that was available was primitive and expensive, costing twenty to thirty dollars a week.

It was necessary to convert a steamer, "The Empire", into a hotel to fill the shortage of rooms to house legislators and other personnel.

As the furor over the lack of facilities grew there was a renewed cry to again move the state's capital.

San Francisco offered whatever buildings the state might need. San Jose tossed in board and room at the bargain rate of $14 a week. And the little town of Benicia said it would give the legislators the use of its Masonic Hall for the Senate, the Presbyterian Church for the Assembly, and a private residence could be used for state offices.

Not to be outdone, Sacramento offered its new two-story courthouse, measuring 50 by 70 feet, along with free tickets to the American Theatre.

It took a number of votes before Sacramento became the accepted site. With little hesitation, Sacramento lobbyists chartered the steamer *Empire* to take the state's legislators the one hundred and ten miles upriver to the new state capital.

The captain of the Empire refused to leave Vallejo until he was paid the $1700 charter fee in advance. The lobbying group came up with the money, and on January 16, 1862, the move from Vallejo to Sacramento was made. California's statehouse finally came to rest.

71

Chapter 11

The Spanish Galleon

(Author's Note: Since the printing of my first book, "Little Known Tales in California History," the author has obtained additional information on the Lost Spanish Galleon. Here, we reprint a revised version of the story)

Many readers justifiably, asked questions about the "Lost Spanish Galleon" tale in our first book, "Little Known Tales in California History". We feel that additional information is needed to clarify that story; information the author did not have in writing his first book.

The question most asked is "How did a seagoing vessel become lost and then sink 100 miles inland from the nearest ocean?

The tale of the lost treasure ship of the southern California desert had its beginnings in 1610. Philip III, reigning King of Spain, ordered sea captain Alvarez de Cordone to arrange for an expedition along the western coast of Mexico in search of pearls.

Cordone's orders were to outfit three ships, two of which were captained by Juan de Iturbe and Pedro de Rosales, while Cordone himself captained the third. Their mission took them to Acapulco, where they requested the importation of sixty experienced pearl divers from Africa.

As the expedition plied the calm coastal waters for pearls, their success was not satisfactory to Cordone. He headed his ships to where he knew the richest beds were, in the Gulf of California

One day, the Spaniards encountered a large Indian village located on the shore. Some of the men were diving for pearls in the shallow coastal waters. Cordone believed he might acquire some fine pearl specimens from the Indians, and ordered the ships to drop anchor.

The Indians proved to be friendly, and Cordone conversed through the night with the Indian chief. The chief told Cordone that the oysters were harvested for food, but when a pearl was found, it was stored and saved for those who fashioned necklaces and other adornments.

When Cordone asked to see the pearls, he was shown more than two-dozen clay pots filled to the brim with the finest stones the sea captain had ever seen. Cordone asked the Indian chief if he would like to trade the pearls for some clothes such as those worn by the Spaniards.

The Indian chief readily agreed, envisioning himself dressed in such finery. An agreement was made and the Spaniards returned to their ships.

The next morning, Cordone deposited several bundles of clothing on the shore in exchange for the pots filled with pearls.

As the precious stones were being transferred to the hold of Iturbe's vessel, the Indians on the shore became enraged. After untying the bundles, they found they had traded their collection of pearls for little more than discarded rags and worn out clothing.

Cordone ordered the sails hoisted, but not before being struck in the chest and felled by an Indian arrow. While the expedition's surgeon worked over Cordone, the vessels managed to sail safely away from the shore. The next day, Cordone's pain and discomfort were such that the surgeon was certain the captain had blood poisoning.

The surgeon convinced the captain that he needed to return to Acapulco for treatment. Before departing for Acapulco, however, Cordone ordered the captains of the other two vessels to continue up the coast into the Gulf of California in search of more pearls.

During their cruise just off the coast of Isla Angel de la Guardia, Rosales's ship struck a reef. Crewmen worked frantically to transfer the cargo of pearls aboard to the vessel of Iturbe. The two captains decided to continue the search for the valuable pearls aboard the lone remaining vessel.

The ship entered an estuary where the Colorado River met the gulf. The Colorado, at the time, carried much greater amounts of water than it does today, and its flow spilled across nearly sixty miles of desert lowlands, forming a huge inland sea. Iturbe and his crew entered the sea in search of more oyster beds.

After exploring the inland sea for two weeks, Iturbe and his crew found little more than a shallow accumulation of overflow from the Colorado River. When Iturbe navigated his vessel back to the point where he had entered the inland sea, he discovered a low ridge of land separating the sea from the gulf. The galleon was hopelessly landlocked.

Geologists believed an earthquake hit the area, causing a subtle shifting of the continental plate, creating a change in the topography.

Distressed with his situation, Iturbe sailed back into the shallow sea in search of an outlet to the gulf. Not only was the ship trapped a hundred miles from the gulf, but due to the intense evaporation taking place, as the Colorado was no longer feeding water into the sink, the level of the sea lowered at a rapid rate.

Eventually, the ship's hull became lodged on the sandy bottom. Taking what they could carry, the sea captains and the crewmen struck out across the desert sand toward the gulf. Months later a Spanish vessel near the present-day coastal town of Guaymas picked up the survivors.

For more than two centuries, the treasure-laden galleon lay on the desert floor, sometimes covered and other times exposed by the shifting sand. There have been many well-organized searches for the galleon without success. There have been some who claim the vessel was haunted and only appeared at certain times of the year.

In 1892, a party of prospectors traveling near Superstition Mountain discovered a long mast timber lying on the desert floor, partially covered by drifting sand.

In 1915, an aged Yuma Indian arrived at the town of Indio and attempted to purchase food with a handful of small shiny round stones. A local businessman realized the stones were actually pearls.

The Indian described coming upon a strangely shaped "wooden house" partially covered by sand. Inside the house, he had discovered many wood cases containing thousands of the small rose and cream-colored stones.

The excited Indio businessman offered the Indian several hundred dollars to lead him to the site of the "wooden house". The Indian agreed and accepted the offer of the businessman to lodge at his home for the night. In the morning, the Indian had vanished.

Indians, Spaniards, Mexicans and American prospectors have told stories about the great ship seen lying in the Imperial Valley desert sands. Many geographers deny that the valley held water during the period of Spanish exploration and conquest, but the myth of the lost Spanish Galleon refuses to die.

Many men have been convinced the ship really exists, and have searched the valley and the surrounding desert for the vessel. There is one miner named Charley Clusker, who claimed in 1870 to have found the vessel.

Charley was a veteran of many desert and mountain adventures, whom, at 60 years of age, talked two men into bankrolling his first search for the phantom craft. This attempt failed, but Charley, undaunted, headed into the desert again with three new companions.

They claimed to have found the rotting hulk on this second try. Reports of the find seemed highly exaggerated, some describing the ship as 200 feet long and decorated with ornate crosses and filled with gold doubloons and pearls.

Charley then led a third expedition back into the desert, all loaded with picks, shovels and other salvage implements. After being gone a suspiciously long time, the searchers returned empty-handed, claiming their animals had worn out, forcing them to turn back.

Skeptics doubt that Charley ever found the lost Spanish galleon, but since his companions were financing the searches, it provided him a grubstake to cover as much gold country as possible

While Charley moved on to chase other golden dreams, the Lost Ship of the Desert entered Western lore as an unsolved mystery.

The sea was filled again when the Colorado River broke and reflooded the valley, creating what is now the existing Salton Sea. The sea level is maintained today strictly by irrigation runoff and what little precipitation falls in that portion of the desert.

There are treasure seekers who return to the area in hopes of finding an exposed bow or stern of the old ship, hoping that the constantly shifting sands will one day uncover the mystery galleon.

Chapter 12

The Battle of the Bees

In 1867, honeybees were scarce in San Diego. The industrious insect was not native to America. Like the horse, the honeybee originated and propagated in Europe, Asia and Africa.

Explorers did bring both horses and honeybees to America, but honeybees generally kept to the eastern side of the continent. The great American plains, the Rocky Mountains, the southwestern desert, and the humid jungles of southern Mexico were formidable barriers to the honeybee's western progress.

There were two events that occurred in the late 1840s and early 1850s that paved the way for the honeybee's migration to California. One was the discovery of gold, and the other was the invention of the Lanstroth moveable-frame beehive.

Lorenzo Lorraine Langstroth invented the moveable beehive in 1851 in Philadelphia. Before Langstroth's honeybee hive, beekeeping was simply a hobby. Beekeepers, in order to harvest the honey from previous hive designs, were forced to kill the honeybees with sulfur smoke.

Wrote a beekeeper in 1861: "Years ago, the only method practiced of getting honey was by digging a pit, setting a brimstone match in this over which a

78

hive of devoted bees was placed, and the fumes of the burning match would kill the entire colony."

The new honeybee hive transformed beekeeping into an industry. It offered an opportunity for entrepreneurs who could envision riches by bringing the industrious honeybees to California where settlers would pay dearly for a taste of honey.

The problem was in transporting hives of bustling honeybees nearly 6000 miles and still keeping them alive. Several efforts were made to bring honeybees west in the early 1850s, but with little success.

The journey required a hot and humid train ride across the Darien Isthmus (now Panama). Most of the bees died enroute.

It took the enterprising John S. Harbison, a Pennsylvania beekeeper, to accomplish the feat. After months of careful planning, on October 29, 1857, Harbison started on the long journey from Newcastle, Pennsylvania, to Sacramento, California. With him, he brought 67 colonies of honeybees.

Harbison arrived in Sacramento December 2, 1857, thirty-five days after leaving Pennsylvania. Fifty strong colonies of honeybees survived the arduous trip, and the far-sighted Harbison was in business.

His first project after arriving in Sacramento was to increase his apiary herd. By the end of 1858, he sold 130 hives of honeybees for $100 each. In Pennsylvania, each hive would have brought only $9 or $10 each.

With this initial success, Harbison returned east, and he and his brother, William, brought out another shipment. In 1859, the Harbison brothers sold another 284 colonies of bees, again for $100 each.

This sent off a frenzy of bee shipping from the east to California. Beekeeping historian Lee H. Watkins wrote: "During the winter of 1859-60 more than one thousand colonies were shipped from the Mohawk Valley of New York State alone."

One newspaper wrote that hardly a steamer arrives from Panama that did not contain hundreds of hives of honeybees.

During the decade from 1859 to 1868, the honeybee made its way south to Los Angeles and San Bernardino counties. In 1869, a few hives were carted south to San Diego.

A Sweetwater Valley rancher named Richard S. Pardee purchased three of the hives. He concluded that beekeeping had a fine future in San Diego.

Pardee's optimism eventually reached Harbison in Sacramento. Even though he had never been in San Diego, Harbison was so convinced of Pardee's sincerity and integrity that he decided to set up an apiary in San Diego County.

Because of the press of his Sacramento business, Harbison entered into an agreement with Robert G. Clark to operate the San Diego apiary under the name, Clark & Harbison.

Consequently, on November 28, 1869, 110 hives of bees arrived in San Diego. The bees made the voyage from San Francisco aboard the steamship Orizaba in perfect condition.

By the summer of 1871, Clark and Harbison were shipping honey to San Francisco. This prompted them to bring another 154 hives from Sacramento to the San Diego operation in 1871. In 1872 and 1874, an additional 540 hives were added.

Clark and Harbison encouraged others to take up beekeeping. The San Diego Union newspaper noted in its November 22, 1872, issue that Clark and Harbison sold nearly 300 stands of bees to farmers in every part of San Diego County. "Nearly every ranch in San Diego," the newspaper wrote, "is now an apiary on a small scale."

Clark and Harbison's honey became well known for its quality. It won "first premium for the best honey" at the 1872 California State Fair.

The word of California's quality honey spread around the world. A New York newspaper described the California honey as being whiter, of heavier body, and sweeter than eastern honey.

Not everybody in San Diego was fond of the honeybees. Sheep ranchers, then called "wool growers", had been allowed grazing privileges for their sheep without the encumbrance of fences.

Beekeepers petitioned the state legislature for repeal of the "No Fence" law then in existence, because bees also needed lots of forage. The No Fence law permitted grazing over uncultivated land in San Diego County but nowhere else in the state.

One angry beekeeper wrote: "San Diego County is the only place on earth where a man who owns and pays taxes on 160 acres of land has no right to the full and undisturbed possession and use of it." The beekeeper maintained the law allowed sheep and cattlemen to literally eat the beekeepers out of

81

"house and home" provided the land was not in cultivation.

The California Legislature repealed the No Fence law in March 1876.

While the beekeepers won the No Fence battle, there were disgruntled San Diego citizens who didn't appreciate having hordes of honeybees that invaded fruit stores and gardens.

San Diego's Board of Trustees passed an ordinance prohibiting the keep of bees in that part of the city lying south of the San Diego River. Beekeepers, however, paid little mind to the ordinance.

The ignoring of the ordinance by beekeepers brought on a new flood of complaints from citizens. According to the San Diego Union, "Every household in town where fruit is being preserved, and every merchant dealing in honey is completely overrun by these little pests."

Beekeepers finally acquiesced and moved their bees outside of town.

The battle was not finished. Even more vocal than the San Diego citizens were fruit growers outside of town. They went to court to get the apiaries moved away from their orchards.

When the courts were slow to react, fruit growers adopted another tactic, that of night riding. Beekeeper Harbison said in an 1889 letter to the American Bee Journal that arsonists had burned 350 of his beehives. He noted that in addition, he himself had destroyed another 750 hives to satisfy the fruit men.

There was one act that brought new credibility to the buzzing honeybee. In May of 1881, a civic-minded swarm of bees was said to have attacked a six-foot-long rattlesnake and stung it so severely that it was easily killed with a spade.

The economics of the honey industry served to sweeten the acceptance of the honeybees. Honey brought San Diego County some one hundred thousand dollars in 1874, one-tenth of the county's total revenues of one million dollars. The honeybee was in California to stay.

Chapter 13

Tiburcio Vasquez

Tiburcio Vasquez

By the time he was 21-years-old, Tiburcio Vasquez led his own gang of bandits. Even at this young age, he was well on his way to becoming California's master outlaw.

Vasquez, like his contemporary, Joaquin Murietta, was a California legend. But unlike Murietta, who had no police records to document his outlawry, Tiburcio Vasquez was well known on police blotters.

From his early background, Vasquez should never have been a bandit. He was born to a respected family in Monterey on August 11, 1835 (some sources list his birth date as 1839). The Vasquez home was a handsome adobe structure located behind Colton Hall, where California's first Constitutional Convention was held, and which still stands today.

Some historians claim Vasquez got his first push down the road to outlawry through his association with Anastacio Garcia, reputedly a one-time member of a band of outlaws.

Vasquez centered his outlaw activity on the wagon routes leading from Los Angeles to the Cerro Gordo Mines and in the San Joaquin Valley. His final capture was in what is now West Hollywood.

It seems unlikely that Tiburcio would become an outlaw. As a young man, he attended school in Monterey and learned to read and write with proficiency, an accomplishment he was justly proud of all his life.

It was one night in 1852 that Vasquez launched on his criminal career. While attending a *fandango* in Monterey with Anastacio Garcia, Vasquez became embroiled in a melee in which Constable William Hardmount was slain. The young Tiburcio fled to the hills with Garcia. Vasquez claimed his crimes were the result of his hate for the *Norte Americano* who had discriminated against Californians of Spanish and Mexican origin. He hated the gringos for leveling slights and insults at his family origin.

By 1856, Tiburcio had his own gang and was soon considered California's master outlaw. Vasquez specialized in the stealing of horses, making a series of raids on ranches from Monterey County to Los Angeles. The Vasquez gang would rebrand and sell the stolen horses.

After rustling a herd of horses from a ranch near Newhall in Los Angeles County, Vasquez tried to sell them too soon. A sheriff's posse caught him and a companion. When his companion turned state's evidence, Tiburcio was sentenced to five years in San Quentin.

He continued his outlaw activity after his release from prison. Vasquez joined with two other infamous California *bandidos,* Tomas Redondo, alias Procopio or Red-Handed Dick, and the bloodthirsty villain Juan Soto. Their crimes ranged from Sonoma County south into the San Joaquin Valley. Vasquez was in and out of San Quentin three times.

In 1873, Vasquez and his *desperado* companions went too far. In a raid in Tres Pinos, a small town six miles south of Hollister, in San Benito County, three citizens were killed and two hundred dollars in gold was stolen.

News of this murderous escapade made Vasquez a household word throughout northern and central California. Governor Newton Booth offered a thousand-dollar reward for the apprehension of Vasquez.

The bandit realized that northern California was now too hot for him. With two trusted companions, Clodovio Chavez and Abdom Leiva, Vasquez headed south.　Near Buena Vista Lake, Abdom's wife, Rosaria Leiva, joined the trio.

Vasquez Rocks, near Los Angeles, was a favorite hangout of Tiburcio Vasquez.

The group headquartered at Heffner's Ranch, nestled among the pines near tiny Elizabeth Lake in the Antelope Valley.

It was no secret that Vasquez considered himself a ladies' man.　And his amorous intentions toward the comely Rosaria Leiva almost brought about Vasquez's demise.

Abdom Leiva suspected that something was going on between Vasquez and his wife.　When he returned

87

early one day, he found the two in a *"fragrante delicto"*, or sexual embrace.

The enraged Abdom drew his pistol and threatened to shoot Vasquez. Clodovio Chavez dissuaded him from doing so, and Leiva left the camp with his wife, vowing vengeance against Tiburcio at some later time. Leiva left his adulterous wife at the ranch.

True to his word, Leiva rode to Lyon's Station in Soledad Canyon where he surrendered to authorities and readily agreed to turn state's evidence against Vasquez. With the sheriffs of both Monterey and Los Angeles County in hot pursuit of them, Vasquez and Chavez managed to escape.

But with information supplied by Leiva, several Vasquez gang members who had remained in hiding in San Benito and Monterey counties were apprehended.

Vasquez came out of the mountains long enough to get Rosaria at Heffner's ranch. The couple, along with the faithful Clodovio Chavez, rode back into the San Gabriel Mountains. During the time of their seclusion, Rosaria became pregnant.

The outlaw could not stand the weeks of inactivity. In 1873, Vasquez decided to leave his mountain haunt and organize a new outlaw band. The presence of the pregnant Rosaria was now a hindrance to the outlaw. He abandoned her in the mountains, where she was alone and helpless, dispelling any thinking that the bandit was a gallant Robin Hood type folk hero.

Rosaria was later able to make her way out of the wilderness and eventually to her home in San Jose.

On the day after Christmas, 1873, Vasquez and his gang made front-page news by sacking the town of Kingston in Fresno County. They bound victims and relieved them of their valuables, and looted two stores, taking twenty five hundred dollars in cash and jewelry.

This act enraged the sheriffs of Fresno, Tulare, San Joaquin, Santa Clara and Monterey counties, who all organized posses to hunt the Vasquez gang.

The California legislature empowered Governor Newton Booth to spend fifteen thousand dollars to bring Vasquez to justice. In 1874, the governor offered a reward of three thousand dollars for Vasquez alive or two thousand dollars for him dead. A month later, these figures were raised to eight thousand alive and six thousand dead.

Sheriff Harry Morse of Alameda County, capturer of Juan Soto and a host of other desperados, was assigned the task of tracking down Vasquez. With a handpicked posse of deputies, Sheriff Morse set out.

The robber band fled, eventually arriving at the stage station in Coyote Holes. There they fired several shots into the roof and ordered the occupants out. Their victims were lined up, robbed of their valuables, and marched behind a nearby hill and tied up.

Then the gang waited for the late arrival of the Owens Valley stage bound for Los Angeles. Vasquez expected to find a fortune in the strongbox, but instead found only $10,000 in mining stock. This he simply scattered to the wind.

Sheriff Harry Morse hounded Vasquez. His break came when Vasquez went to rob sheep rancher Alexander Repetto, who had sold a large quantity of wool. When Vasquez and his band drew pistols, Repetto could produce a mere eighty dollars.

The puny sum enraged Vasquez. The outlaw ordered Repetto to write a check for $800. Repetto's thirteen-year-old nephew was dispatched to take the check to the Temple and Workman bank in Los Angeles and bring back the cash.

While Vasquez warned the lad that his uncle would be killed if he informed anybody of the gangsters' activity, bank officials nevertheless became suspicious over the youth's nervousness. The officials notified Sheriff Billy Rowland.

The sheep man's nephew had scarcely handed the money over to Vasquez when the outlaw spotted the dust of Sheriff Rowland and his posse. He and his gang again departed for the hills. During the chase, Vasquez' horse stumbled into a steep gully, breaking a leg. Vasquez jumped aboard the horse of another gang member, escaping the law.

But the outlaw's luck was running out. Vasquez made a fatal mistake after the Repetto incident by not fleeing to Mexico as his friends urged him to do.

Law officials, still on Vasquez tail, learned the bandit was hiding in the Cahuenga Mountains (now Hollywood Hills) at the ranch of Greek George. It is believed a former gang member gave the information to the sheriff.

Los Angeles sheriff Billy Rowland dispatched deputy D. K. Smith to stake out Greek George's ranch. Smith disguised himself as a *vaquero* looking for work. Smith hung around the ranch for several days before he spied Vasquez.

This set in motion the actions leading to the capture of the notorious outlaw. The sheriff commandeered a wagon driven by two Mexicans going into the mountains to gather wood. Six deputies hid in the bed of the empty wagon and the Mexicans were ordered to drive up to the ranch house of Greek George.

Vasquez was eating lunch. He sprang to his feet as armed deputies burst through the door. The bandit made a flying leap through the kitchen window into the drawn pistol of George Beers, a reporter for the *San Francisco Chronicle* who was allowed to accompany the lawmen.

Vasquez spent nine days in the Los Angeles jail and became the object of statewide attention. In interviews granted to three reporters, Vasquez insisted he had never killed a man and that his motives were honorable.

In the eight months preceding his trial, Vasquez was transported to the jail in Salinas and charged with the murder of Leander Davidson at Tres Pinos. He was then moved to San Jose to stand trial.

Vasquez continued to be something of a celebrity and even a hero to hundreds of his fellow Spanish-speaking citizens. He seemed to enjoy his notoriety, even autographing and selling photographs taken after his arrest.

His trial for murder was held in January 1875. The trial lasted four days and the jury took two hours to reach a guilty verdict. He met his death by hanging on March 19, 1875, in San Jose.

Clodovio Chavez fled to Yuma, Arizona, where two deputies shot him to death.

The outlaw is still remembered by two place names in southern California. Vasquez Canyon, the Big Tujunga tributary used by the outlaw in his getaway, immortalizes the Repetto Ranch raid. Vasquez Rocks, above Soledad Canyon, is now a Los Angeles County park, and marks one of the bandit's favorite hideouts.

Chapter 14

California's Last Dry Town

A print of Pacific Grove high school appeared on a postcard.

Pacific Grove was proud of its prohibition against alcohol. The town was originally founded as a religious retreat for Methodists wanting to become closer to God by living and worshiping in the beautiful forest that He created.

At the Howard Street Methodist Episcopal Church in San Francisco on June 1, 1875, a group of people held the first meeting of the Pacific Grove Retreat Association. Besides adopting Pacific Grove as the name for the town, there were several other issues to be confronted.

Among the major concerns was the sale of intoxicants. The blue laws, referred to as the "Rules by the Founding Fathers," dealt with some rather diverse subjects. They included things such as the behavior that would be allowed on the grounds, the delivery of baggage on Sundays, staying out past 10:30 p.m., smoking on platforms or near public buildings, cursing, and walking around clad only in a bathing suit.

The provisions concerning alcohol were particularly strict. The laws adopted set forth the following:

INTOXICANTS: The buying, selling, or giving away of any and all intoxicants – spirituous liquors, wine, beer, or cider – are strictly prohibited on any public or private property within one mile of the center of the original survey of the Retreat and Directors request all well disposed persons to promptly notify the superintendent of any violations of this rule.

Even those buying property had to agree to a provision in the lease that prohibited the sale of liquor on the property. This clause also prohibited gambling on such property.

As Pacific Grove grew, many of the blue laws adopted by its founding fathers began to disappear. However, the town continued to enforce its prohibition against the sale of alcohol within the city limits.

The town became known as the "Chautauqua-by-the-Sea", a community of culture and learning. The first camp meeting of the Pacific Coast branch of the

95

Chautauqua Literary and Scientific Circle was held in 1879.

The event was fashioned after the Methodist Sunday school teachers' training camp established in 1874 at Lake Chautauqua, N.Y.

Pacific Grove built Chautauqua Hall in 1881, which became known as the Old Chapel or Assembly Hall. This hall could hold 500 people during the summer. In the winter, it was used to store tents and other gear.

Speakers came from all over the world to lecture at what became a well-known cultural center in the west. At the end of each season, the town held its "Feast of Lanterns", which signified the closing of each Chautauqua until the next summer.

In November 1879, after the summer campers returned home, Robert Louis Stevenson wandered into the deserted campgrounds: "I have never been in any place so dreamlike. Indeed, it was not so much like a deserted town as like a scene upon the stage by daylight, and with no one on the boards."

Pacific Grove's last Chautauqua was held in August 1926.

It wasn't until 1927 that Pacific Grove Retreat decided to become a legitimate town. Thirteen people were elected to write a charter, which was duly approved by both the California legislature and by the voters of the Pacific Grove Retreat.

Residents of Pacific Grove learned that the city's strict control over the sale of alcohol was hurting them economically. Tourists were welcome visitors to the Monterey Bay area, and their dollars were important, even to Pacific Grove.

Many of the tourists, not able to relax with a glass of wine at dinner, simply drove to neighboring towns outside the dry area, such as Monterey, Watsonville or Santa Cruz for dinner.

Soon, the tourists began staying at hotels in towns that allowed the sale of alcohol, alleviating the necessity of driving back to Pacific Grove after dinner.

It didn't take Pacific Grove's city fathers long to realize they were losing money to surrounding communities because of the ban on alcohol. Residents began holding meetings to discuss the need to legalize alcohol.

Strong campaigns emerged to abolish the "no alcohol" law. Merchants felt they were at a great disadvantage with their neighboring communities, especially Monterey, which was their main competitor.

The Monterey Herald reported, "There are no bars, liquor stores, nor cocktail lounges in Pacific Grove and there may never be any. The original deed restrictions provided for a town whose lips would never touch liquor."

Leading the fray to keep Pacific Grove dry was Mrs. Elmarie Dyke, who moved to Pacific Grove with her family in 1909. Mrs. Dyke graduated from Pacific Grove high school, and later became a schoolteacher in the city's schools. She also reinstated and produced the Feast of Lanterns from 1963 until 1980.

Her strong determination was not enough to keep alcohol out of Pacific Grove.

Pacific Grove Mayor Bob Quinn noted at one meeting that Pacific Grove residents didn't drink any less than their neighbors. There were just as many liquor bottles in the trash in Pacific Grove, but the people just could not buy it there.

Finally, in 1968, the City of Pacific Grove decided to vote on the issue of whether the laws barring alcohol should be repealed. The measure passed easily on a vote of 3383 to 2269.

Even today the consumption of alcohol in public places in Pacific Grove is restricted to sit-down restaurants where food is served. Liquor can be purchased, however, at a limited number of closely monitored package stores.

Chapter 15

The Naming of California

California was named Queen Califia.

There is considerable controversy over who first applied the name California to the land that was once thought to be an island in the Pacific.

Historians seem to feel the name was derived from a second-rate Spanish novel, *"Las Sergas de Esplandian"*, written about 1500 by Garci Ordonez de Montalvo.

The novel is described as being a rather decadent book about one of those impossible romances of chivalry, including King Arthur and his Round Table. Its hero was Esplandian, a perfect knight, sworn to follow in his father's footsteps as *conquistador* of all his enemies.

In the novel, California appears as the name of a wonderful island of tall, bronze-colored Amazon women, ruled by a pagan called *"Queen Califia"*. The fact that these women repelled all male suitors excited the Spanish imagination.

Most historians credit the explorer Francisco de Bolanos with naming California. Bolanos explored the coast above the tip of Lower California in 1541, a year before the expedition of Juan Rodriguez Cabrillo.

The earliest authenticated record of the use of the name *California* by explorers is in the journal of the Cabrillo expedition, but there it appears as a name already in common usage.

In his novel *Las Sergas de Esplandian*, Montalvo uses the following descriptions of his fictional island:

"Know ye that at the right hand of the Indies there is an island named California, very close to that part of the Terrestrial Paradise. which is inhabited by black women, without a single man among them, and they lived in the manner of Amazons. They were robust of body, with strong and passionate hearts and great virtues. The island itself is one of the wildest in the world on account of the bold and craggy rocks. Their weapons were all made of gold. The island everywhere abounds with gold and precious stones, and upon it no other metal was found. They lived in caves, well excavated. They had many ships with which they sailed to other coasts to make forays, and the men whom they took as prisoners they killed. In this island, named California, there are many griffins. In no other part of the world can they be

101

found. And there ruled over that island of California a queen of majestic proportions, more beautiful than the others, and in the very vigor of her womanhood. She is desirous of accomplishing great deeds. She was valiant and courageous, and ardent, with a brave heart, and had ambitions to execute nobler actions than had been performed by any other ruler."

The earliest maps bearing the name California vary as to the exact area to which the name was applied. The name California was first applied to the southern part of Lower California, probably in 1533-34, but at any rate before 1542.

By extension, it was applied in the plural to the entire Pacific coast north from Cape San Lucas. The region was known by several names in the first years of its discovery, but the one, which was ultimately retained, is probably the most melodious.

In 1579, Sir Francis Drake repaired his ships in Drake's Bay, and named the land New Albion. Spanish galleons enroute from the Philippines to Acapulco usually sighted the coast, and certainly did so in the voyages of 1584 and 1595.

Most of this time, California was generally supposed to be an island or a group of islands.

In Montalvo's novel, Queen Calafia and her tribe of Amazons trapped the griffins while they were small. They fed the griffins with the men whom they took as prisoners, and with the boys to whom they gave birth.

Montalvo ended by having Queen Calafia convert to Christianity, and even gaining a proper respect for men. She finally married a relative of Esplandian, and returned with him to California.

Chapter 16

Those Pony Express Boys

While the Pony Express, established in April 1860, was a financial failure, it did indeed serve a noble purpose. The Pony Express proved to the eastern establishment that the Central Route could be used by railroads to bind the country together.

The Pony Express is credited with keeping California in the Union at a time when General Albert Sydney Johnston, then military commander of California, was believed to be leaning toward siding with the Confederacy.

A message was dispatched by the Pony Express to President Lincoln regarding Johnston's loyalty. Lincoln immediately sent Brigadier General Edwin Sumner to relieve Johnston of his duties.

There were about 80 Pony Express riders in use at any one time. In addition to the riders, there were 400 other employees needed as station keepers, stock tenders and route superintendents.

The Pony Express was patterned after the horseback relay mail service that dates back to thirteenth-century China, where post stations were located twenty-five miles apart.

In 1845, it took U.S. President James K. Polk six months to get a message to California. After the Gold Rush brought thousands of Americans to the far west, getting the mail from coast to coast became an increasingly important need.

Later on, when mail service contracts were given to stagecoach companies, The famous Butterfield's Overland Mail Company carried mail from Fort Smith, Arkansas, to San Francisco in three to four weeks. Mail carried by overland stage from St. Louis to San Francisco took 24 days.

William H. Russell, of the freighting firm of Russell, Majors & Waddell, created the Pony Express.

When first placed into operation the Pony Express carried the mail once a week in each direction, east and west. During the Paiute Indian War in May 1860 many of the stations and a large portion of the equipment between Salt Lake City and Carson City, Nevada, were destroyed and the operation was suspended.

After the cessation of the Paiute Indian War, the mail continued being carried by the Pony Express, twice a week in each direction. The delivery time was generally 10 days from St. Joseph to San Francisco, although later trips were made in eight or nine days.

When Abraham Lincoln was elected President of the United States, his inaugural address was carried from St. Joseph, Missouri, to Sacramento in seven days, 17 hours.

Financially, the Pony Express did not pay back its investors. For one thing, Congress never got around to paying Russell, Majors and Waddell for services rendered. The firm had been surviving on loans made against its government debts since 1858. The company was essentially bankrupt.

Although the Pony Express was an efficient mail service, it failed as a profitable enterprise. It is not known exactly how much the service cost Russell, Majors and Waddell, but during its operation the company grossed only $90,141, or about the cost of purchasing horses for the service. Some accounts placed the Pony Express losses at $200,000 by the time it ceased operations.

Pony Express riders were first paid $50 per month, plus room and board. This pay soon rose to about $100 to $125 per month. Riders on particularly dangerous routes received $150.

William "Sam" Hamilton was the first eastbound rider out of Sacramento on April 4th, 1860

Hamilton covered the 45 miles from Sacramento to Placerville in four hours. Changing horses in Placerville, he was off to Sportsmans Hall twelve miles away. He made it in one hour, finishing his first ride.

Warren Upson had the assignment of traversing the worst section of trail on the entire Pony Express route. The road was upgrade, steep in many places, and wound up through the rugged Sierra Nevada Mountains.

Warren "Boston" Upson carried the dangerous second leg from Sportsman's Hall in Pollock Pines over the Sierras to Friday's Station on the shores of Lake Tahoe.

Normally, the Washoe Road was clogged with wagon traffic, but Upson's first ride found the trail covered with deep snow that persisted all the way to Woodfords. His route took him through the pines and snow to BrocklissBridge, a toll crossing over the South Fork of the American River.

His horse clattered across the toll bridge and climbed up the north side of the canyon. Upson changed horses at Moss', Webster's and Strawberry, and made a treacherous river crossing at Slippery Ford.

The young rider crossed Johnson's Summit (7382 feet elevation) in a driving snowstorm. Upson urged his pony south over Luther Pass (7740 feet) in the driving snowstorm. The trail then dropped 1300 feet during the steep two-mile descent to the Upper Truckee River.

A westbound rider had an equally difficult ride, according to a report in the *Sacramento Daily Union*, April 16, 1860. From the Sierra Nevada summit the grade narrows to ten feet wide for a stretch of nearly two miles.

Late in the afternoon, a large pack train had started down the mountain, but the soft snow forced the drivers to stop when half way down the grade. The drivers removed the packs from the mules and left both the packs and the mules in the trail. The drivers walked back to the summit to spend the night.

When Pony Express rider Upson reached the grade about midnight, he encountered the mules and their loads of goods.

There was but one way to pass, and that was to break a path for his horse around each mule. It took him three-and-a-half hours, but he finally accomplished the task without slipping off the precipice. That day the Pony Express mail arrived in Sacramento too late to catch the boat to San Francisco.

The Pony Express lasted only 19 months, ending when the Transcontinental Telegraph Line was completed in October 1861.

Ironically, Samuel F. B. Morse, inventor of the telegraph, had been working on the idea years before the Pony Express began. On September 21, 1837, Morse petitioned Congress for funds to build a practical working telegraph.

Lawmakers weren't interested. England, Russia and France likewise refused him funds. It wasn't until 1843, after a six-year delay, that Congress finally granted funds, and in 1844 Morse's telegraph linked Baltimore and Washington.

Chapter 17

Bodie Was Wild and Wooly

The Bodie Methodist Church

Bodie was never a tame town. As soon as the miners finished a long day in the mines, they headed for the bars and the red light district to spend their earnings.

It has been said that a killing occurred in Bodie every day, making the undertaker one of the more prosperous businessmen in town.

Bodie is located on the eastern side of the Sierras, north of Mono Lake and a few miles west of the

Nevada border. It sits at 8,379 feet elevation. Waterman S. Body (or Bodye, Bodie, or Bodey) and three companions discovered gold west of the present town site in 1859. A mining district was organized on July 10, 1860.

There is considerable controversy as to why the town was spelled "Bodie". Most authorities seem to agree that it was a deliberate change by town residents to insure proper pronunciation of the camp's name.

The town boasted a railroad, the "Bodie and Benton", which, an observer said, was a railroad essentially between "nowhere and nowhere". Bodie was a wild town and it wasn't unusual for a resident to be called a "Bad Man from Bodie". The town itself was frequently called "Shooters Town".

Citizens boasted that Bodie had the widest streets, the meanest men, the worst climate, and the most disgusting whiskey in the west. Virgin Alley and Maiden Lane had neither.

It was often said that a "hanging or a church will kill any mining town". Bodie had both and much more. A local preacher called the town a "sea of sin lashed by tempests of lust and passion."

Most of the whorehouses were located along Virgin Alley, where such demimondes as Big Bonanza, Beautiful Doll, Big Nell, Bull Con Josie, and Rosa May plied the oldest of all professions.

The *Reno Weekly Gazette*, in 1879, wrote that Bodie had more saloons in a given length than any thoroughfare in the world.

111

Lack of capital forced the sale and consolidation of claims during 1861-1862. One result was the formation of the Bodie Bluff Consolidated Mining Company, with Leland Stanford as president.

When the company failed, the Empire Company of New York took control, but it failed, too. It seemed as if Bodie's death was inevitable.

This community of houses still stands in the Bodie ghost town.

In 1876, the Bodie mine was developed and the town was revitalized. By 1879, the population was 10,000 plus. Other mines, such as the Standard and Bulmer, became good producers. During the late 1870s and most of the 1880s, Bodie became one of the richest mining camps in the west.

112

The need for wood for fuel in the mines required 45,000 cords per year. Many of the wood camp laborers were Chinese. It is claimed that at one time, Bodie had a larger Chinese population than any other settlement in California except San Francisco.

The town's founder met an unfortunate end shortly after discovering gold. He headed for Monoville in the autumn of 1859 to stock up on supplies for the winter.

On the return trip, he and E.S. Taylor were caught in a blizzard, and Body became exhausted. Taylor left his partner wrapped in a blanket and went for help. When he returned to where he thought he had left his companion, there was no trace of Body.

Bodie School House

The following spring his body was found, taken to Bodie and laid to rest on the hill overlooking the town site.

But Body's body was not destined to rest. *The Daily Free Press* reported on December 3, 1879, that *"Someone left the gate of the cemetery open last night and let in a terrible draft of cold air. It was so cold that Bill Bodey (sic) got up and shut the gate with such a slam that both hinges were broken off. The residents of that section state that his language, on the occasion, was frightful."*

It was probably about this time that the settlement was named, or renamed, in his honor.

The town blossomed to about 20,000 residents by 1878. There were sixty saloons, a number of gambling halls, several breweries, and five newspapers to serve the thriving mining town.

Things were never dull for Bodie town officials. For instance consider the following letter to city hall:

KIND AND RESPECTED CIR:---I see in the paper that a man named John Sipes was attacted and et up by a bare whose kubs he was trying to get when that she bare came up and stopt him by eating him in the mountains near your town.

What I want to know is did it kill him ded or was he only partly et up and is he from this place and all about the bar. I don't know but he is a distant husband of mine. My first

114

husband was of that name and I
supposed he was killed in the war, but
the name of the man the bare et being
the same I thought it might be him all
and I ought to know if he wasn't killed
either in the war or by the bare, for I
have been married twice and there
ought to be divorse papers got out by
him or me if the bare did not eat him
up. If it is him you will know by his
having six toes on his left foot.

He also had a "spread eagle"
tattooed on his front chest and a anker
on his right arm which you will know
him by if the bare did not eat up these
sines of it being him.

Find out all you kin about hime
without him knowing what it is for,
that is if the bare did not eat him all
up. If it did I don't see as you kin do
anything and you needn't to trouble.

Please ancer back.

P.O.---Was the bare killed? Also
was he married again and did he have
propty wuth me laying claim to?

By 1883, Bodie had begun to decline, with all but
two mines being forced to close. When the mines
died, so did the town, along with the churches, red-
light district, newspaper, and general store. Most
inhabitants simply walked away, leaving homes and

115

businesses as though they were due back at the end of the day.

Gold production did continue until 1955 and in 1962 the State Department of Parks and Recreation was handed the responsibility of administering Bodie as a State Historic Park. The 170 buildings that remain are in a state of arrested decay. Visitors today can walk through the town and peek through tattered lace curtains and discoloring glass and see sagging bedsprings, dusty clothing, and store shelves still filled with merchandise. There is no smoking anywhere in Bodie because of the risk of fire.

Bodie is situated some 8,000 feet above sea level, on a flat extent of rocky terrain exposed on all sides to icy blasts of winter's wind. Bodie is said to be typical of all the ghost towns that once flourished along the gold dust trails in California and Nevada.

Chapter 18

Women Fight to Vote

Susan B. Anthony in California.

Women in California didn't get the right to vote until 1911. It seems somewhat ironic that one of the least populated states, Wyoming, in 1869, was the first to grant women voting rights, years before other states.

With Wyoming's approval of voting rights for women, the way was paved for women in other states to campaign for equal rights. A year after Wyoming's vote, California women convened in San Francisco to organize statewide groups, which would then be affiliated with national groups.

Such suffragist leaders as Susan B. Anthony and Elizabeth Cady Stanton stumped in California in 1871, but California women did not get voting rights for four more decades.

Woman Suffrage is simply the right of women to vote in political elections. Women began demanding suffrage for themselves as early as the 1600s.

It was New Zealand, in 1893, which became the first country to grant women the right to vote in national elections. An organized movement on behalf of suffrage, led by women but also open to men, first emerged in the United States in 1848. The women organizers often met hostility and even violence.

One reason that women's enfranchisement took so long to achieve is that they had to persuade the male electorate to grant them the right to vote. Many men, and some women, believed that women were not suited by circumstance or temperament for the vote.

Many men considered women, by nature, were to be dependent on men and subordinate to them. Many even thought that women could not be trusted to be independent, unswayed by appeals from employers, landlords, or an educated elite.

Women also faced the opposition of powerful politicians who feared that once given the right to vote, the ladies would put them out of office.

The majority of men voting in the California election of 1896 opposed a measure to amend the state constitution in favor of woman suffrage. Finally, in 1911, the male voters came around, and California became the sixth state in the nation to grant voting rights to women.

In the United States, approval of the suffrage movement progressed as follows: Wyoming 1869; Utah 1893; Colorado 1893; Idaho 1896; California 1911; and the balance of the USA, 1920.

Overnight, 400,000 women were eligible to vote equally with men, on all levels, whether it be a school election or one elect a President.

Women's' voting rights didn't come easy in California. A massive distribution of information to the press was masterminded both from northern and southern California prior to the 1911 election.

"We printed ten thousand columns in the daily papers," said Mrs. David C. McCann, president of the Southern California Women's Press Club. "In all ways our campaign was persistent, consistent, (and) insistent. We sent suffrage matter to poultry papers, farmers' journals, and always sent a personal letter. We interviewed every prominent person in the state, and those who came here temporarily."

Equally determined was Elizabeth Lower Watson, president of the California Woman Suffrage Association, who, in 1911, said:

"I am making the plea for woman suffrage on the ground of simple justice only. Are not women equally concerned in pure food, pure air and clean cities physically as well as morally; are not the women interested in parks, public gardens, the building and maintaining of churches and schools?"

Before approval, women were denied admission to all existing U.S. colleges before Oberlin College admitted them, with limitations in 1833. California State Colleges admitted women in the 1870s, but state affiliated schools of law and medicine considered their institutions a special case and refused admission of women.

Even women teachers with equal education earned only one-fourth to one-half as much in salary as their male counterparts doing the same work.

Among the strongest opposition to woman suffrage movement were the liquor interests, believing that women would wage a strong campaign to support the prohibition of alcohol.

Clara Shortridge Foltz and Laura de Force Gordon both led the successful effort in Sacramento in 1878 to change the law that prohibited women from practicing law. Because of their efforts, Hastings School of Law was forced to admit women.

Even as late as 1922, the Supreme Court upheld ineligibility for citizenship by Asians. Asians and other minorities suffered voting and citizenship discrimination well into recent times.

Many of the glaring inequities addressed by suffrage arguments related to family life. Legal guardianship resided with a child's father or other male relative. Married women's signatures on contracts were not binding.

As late as 1916 in California, a husband automatically inherited all his wife's property at her death, whereas she inherited only a portion of their mutual possessions, and only at the discretion of a probate court.

Susan B. Anthony, along with some dozen other women, registered to vote for the election of 1871. The following day, forty more woman registered. On Election Day, fifteen of the women succeeded in voting.

Susan B. was arrested and found guilty. She was ordered to pay a fine of one hundred dollars. Her reply to the judge, "May it please your honor, I will never pay a dollar of your unjust penalty."

The fine remains unpaid to this day.

Chapter 19

State Gem Is Rare

A benitoite specimen.

California's official state gemstone is rare indeed! It's only significant source is a tiny mine in southern San Benito County near the town of Coalinga.

The gemstone is benitoite (pronounced (ben-ee-toe-ite") and was discovered in San Benito County in 1907. When first found, it was believed to be sapphire. After careful examination by mineralogists, it was determined that it was not sapphire. The prized crystal benitoite was named for the county in which it was found.

Benitoite is described as containing the blue color of the sapphire but at the same time having the fire of a diamond. It is in high demand for both gemstones and as specimens.

In terms of scarcity, benitoite is placed on the same level as gem red beryl and a few other rare stones, such as Alexandrite, and is considerably rarer than the diamond.

Due to its rarity, the gem is expensive ($700/ct or more for good quality small stones under 0.20 ct)

Benitoite will never be widely available, as the original deposit has been completely worked out.

While there may be a minor amount of material gained from reworking the tailings from the Benitoite Gem Mine, from which the largest source was obtained, the amount left is expected to be small.

When first discovered, benitoite created an immediate sensation among gemologists because of its well-formed textbook crystals, accompanied by equally striking crystals of neptunite.

The more popular color for benitoite is a rich sapphire blue. Other colors include clear, white, pink, or greenish-gray in color.

It has been found that by heating the blue stones it will sometimes produce a pleasant orange-like color. When this process is successful, these orangy benitoites will command about twice the price as the typical blue ones.

Neither the origin of the color in benitoite nor the person who discovered it is definitely known.

Benitoite does contain traces of iron. One mineralogist, Joan Mamarella, suggests in a thesis that the blue color is derived from titanium located in the blue portions of the crystals.

As for the discoverer of benitoite, one account holds that a Mr. Hawkins and T. Edwin Sanders discovered benitoite in 1907. Other accounts place the discovery at the hands of James Marshall Couch on February 22, 1907.

A book, "The Benitoite Story", was self-published in 1988 by Mr. Couch's step-grandson, David Howard Austin.

In "The Benitoite Story," Couch's discovery is described as follows:

After crossing the creek, he climbed uphill several yards through the thick brush. After removing the brush cover that screened the entrance to two narrow clefts in the hillside, James walked into a fantasy scene. It was as if he had stepped into a giant geode. Before him, poured out at his feet in the dirt with no regard for their value, were literally thousands of multi-hued but mostly beautiful sapphire-blue gems, weathered from the nearly snow-white walls, and the natural matrix of their mother rock. The white walls were studded everywhere with thousands more of the glittering gems still in place, as if growing and ready to be harvested.

Benitoite is found in several locations around the world but only in San Benito County is it found in anything resembling good crystal form. To date, it has been found in four different mines in southern San Benito County, all located relatively closely to each other.

Benitoite was declared the official California State gemstone in 1985.

Chapter 20

Those Fantastic Cable Cars

Andrew Smith Hallidie, inventor of the cable car.

The father of the San Francisco cable car was a Scotsman named Andrew Smith Hallidie. Before inventing the cable car, Hallidie owned a cable manufacturing plant on the corner of Mason and Chestnut streets.

His high quality cable, each strand had a thickness of .062 inch and the completed cable had a tensile strength of 160,000 pounds. Hallidie's cables were used in a number of ways.

Hallidie's wire rope was used in the designing and building of a suspension bridge across the American River. It was also a mainstay in California's gold mines to pull heavy ore cars out of the underground mines.

Hallidie witnessed a horse-drawn streetcar slide backwards under its heavy load while climbing one of San Francisco's steep streets. The heavily weighted wagon slid down the slippery grade, dragging five horses to their death.

After witnessing the gruesome accident, Hallidie was convinced his strong cables could be used to replace the horse-drawn streetcars.

The Scotsman made no secret of his desire to eliminate the use of horses. He would place his strong cables underground and power them with steam. Cars would be attached to the cables much like ore buckets in the mines of the Sierra Nevada gold fields.

Hallidie found an unusual alliance to support his idea to build a cable car that would carry passengers up and down the steep San Francisco hillsides. The support came from the Society for the Prevention of Cruelty to Animals, who claimed that pulling the horse-drawn trams significantly shortened the life of the animals.

Hallidie also gained the support of three friends, Henry Davis, James Moffatt, and Joseph Britton, who could envision Hallidie's description of his cable railway.

A San Francisco Cable Car

The four men, in 1872, formed a corporation and obtained a franchise to build a street railway in Clay Street. Although they offered stock in the corporation to the public, money was slow in materializing.

Eventually, Hallidie himself put up $20,000 for the venture. His partners added another $40,000. The Clay Street Bank, in which the corporation maintained its office, advanced another $30,000.

The partners faced a strict deadline to complete the system. The franchise to build the system was due to expire in one year, on August 1, 1873. The design for the system presented the greatest obstacle.

The working parts of the power system required grips, brakes, trucks for the trams, and other safety features

The greatest obstacle facing the quartet was designing the patterns for the working parts of the power system, the grips, brake, and truck for the trams. The design had dealt also with the suspension, carriage and propulsion of the cable.

The deadline date drew ever closer for the cable car builders. The slot to hold the cable was completed only two days before the experimental run was scheduled.

A powerhouse had been built at the corner of Clay and Leavenworth streets, a full city block beyond the point designated as the terminus for the line. The cable drums were activated by steam engines fired by great Scotch boilers. After 1906, electricity was used to power the cable drums.

The first run for San Francisco's first cable car was set for five o'clock in the morning on the same day the franchise expired. It was a foggy morning, and many of the spectators feared the cable car's brakes would not hold on the rails that were wet from the drizzling fog.

The fog shrouded the area and muffled the sounds spectators expected to hear. Then, as if magically, the mists rolled away, and at the farthest terminus of the line a cable car appeared, upright and intact.

Hallidie's experimental run was completed. His next worry was to conduct a run in which paying passengers rode the new mechanical marvel. Word spread around the city that the cable car was an overwhelming success.

Another run, this time with passengers was set for the afternoon and would include city dignitaries.

Hallidie adapted a passenger car with lateral banquettes or benches to be towed behind the power-governed dummy.

The seating capacity of the dummy and the trailer was only 25 persons. But when the cable car started on that initial run everyone wanted to share the ride. Ninety persons jammed aboard. Over-crowding of cable cars exist today, as city folks and tourists alike clamber aboard already full cars.

The popularity of the cable cars sent the company's stock spiraling, even though the fare was only five cents. The original sixty thousand-dollar investment was earning three thousand dollars every thirty days, better than sixty percent per annum.

Chapter 21

Black Bart, A Poetic Bandit

Black Bart planned and executed his robberies with careful research and undeniable finesse.

During his forays on stagecoaches, the bandit worked alone and left few clues for lawmen to follow. After two robberies, Wells Fargo detectives found bits of poetry in the empty discarded Wells Fargo strong boxes. The poems were signed: *"Black Bart, the PO8."*

In his robberies, he wore a flour-sack over his head, atop of which was perched a derby hat. "Throw down the box," he would roar to the driver. While he collected the loot from the strong boxes, Black Bart never bothered to take the valuables of the passengers.

A Wells-Fargo black box sought by bandits.

When one panicked lady tossed him her purse, Black Bart handed it back to her with the reply, "Thank you madam, but I don't need your money. I only want Wells Fargo's."

The bandit used a number of aliases, including Charles F. Bolton. Charles E. Boles was his true name.

His first stage robbery was on a mountain pass called Funk Hill, four miles outside of Copperopolis in Calaveras County on July 26, 1875. The driver of the stagecoach, John Shine, who was later an U.S. marshal and a California state senator, tossed Bart the wooden box reinforced with iron bands.

Black Bart

The outlaw grabbed the box and hurried into the trees. Being a curious person, stage driver Shine drove a short distance, stopped his stage, and then walked back to the scene of the robbery. He soon was staring into a half-dozen guns leveled at him from behind boulders.

Shine stood rock still. He then realized the outlaws were not moving. When he approached one, he found it was simply a dummy with a stick for a gun. This became a usual method for Black Bart. He would stop a stage, pretending to have an outlaw gang supporting him. He would shout out, "If he dares to shoot, give him a solid volley, boys!"

135

REWARD!

WELLS, FARGO & CO.'S EXPRESS BOX, CON-
taining $100 in Gold Notes, was robbed this morning, by one man, on the route from Sonora
to Milton, near top of the Hill, between the river and Copperopolis.

$250

And one-fourth of any money recovered, will be paid
for arrest and conviction of the robber

JOHN J. VALENTINE,
San Francisco, July 27, 1875. General Sup't.

In one empty strong box, this piece of poetry was found:

"Here I lay me down to sleep
To wait the coming morrow.
Perhaps success, perhaps defeat
And everlasting sorrow.
Yet come what will, I'll try it once,
My conditions can't be worse,
And if there's money in that box,
Tis money in my purse."

While he robbed, Black Bart didn't rob frequently. There was as much as nine months between holdups. He later told lawmen he "took only what was needed when it was needed."

While Bart held up stages as far north as the Oregon border, he concentrated his efforts in the gold country of the Sierra Nevadas. From the time of his first holdup, Black Bart was credited by lawmen with stopping 28 stages over an eight-year period.

To say the least, the bandit had local sheriffs, Wells Fargo detectives and U.S. Postal authorities in a fiery rage. He stopped the stagecoaches while they were traveling along mountainous roads where the driver was compelled to slow down at dangerous curves.

On November 3, 1883, the Sonora stage was rolling along toward Copperopolis, carrying a lone passenger. The passenger was a young boy with a rifle, who told the driver he wanted to do some hunting. He asked the driver to pick him up on the other side of the hill.

When the boy disappeared, Black Bart appeared, and confronting the stage driver, gave his usual order, "Throw down the box."

As a precaution against just such a holdup, the driver had bolted the strong box to the floor of the passenger compartment. When Bart found the strong box was attached to the floor and would take longer to open, he ordered the driver to take the horses over the hill out of sight.

As the driver was doing so, he met the boy with the rifle coming back around the hill. The two hurried back as Black Bart was scrambling into the brush with the loot. The boy sent three shots at the outlaw, wounding him in the hand.

Bart used a handkerchief to wrap around his wound. Lawmen later found the bloodied handkerchief, which had a San Francisco laundry mark on it. One of the detectives assigned to track down Black Bart was Henry Nicholson Morse, one-time sheriff of Alameda County.

Morse faced an arduous task. He had the robber's handkerchief with the laundry mark, FX07, but he soon learned there were ninety-one laundries in San Francisco. He was determined to visit every one of them if necessary.

At Ferguson and Bigg's California Laundry, Morse struck pay dirt. He found the laundry mark belonged to Charles E. Bolton, a mining engineer. Morse arrested Bolton in his hotel room, but when booked, Bolton gave his name as T. Z. Spaulding

In the hotel room, detectives found a Bible that was given to Charles E. Boles by his wife in 1865. Born and raised in upper New York State, Boles had been a farmer, and later served as a sergeant in the 116th Illinois Volunteer Infantry just before the Civil War. The lawmen's investigation left them assured that it Boles who was the much wanted Black Bart.

When Boles' family members died, he headed to California where he briefly panned for gold and worked a few other odd jobs before turning to stagecoach robbery.

Records show that Black Bart (Boles) invested his loot in several small business ventures that provided him a modest income. As money became short, he would return to stagecoach holdups.

For days after his arrest, Boles denied being the famous Black Bart. He finally did admit to several robberies, but only those occurring before 1879. He mistakenly believed he was protected by the statute of limitations for those holdups.

Black Bart was convicted January 21, 1888. He was sentenced to six years in San Quentin. This was shortened to four years for good behavior. By the time of his release, he was aging considerably, with both his eyesight and his hearing beginning to fail.

As he left the prison, his spirit seemed crushed. He hurried to escape the newsmen that surrounded him when he stepped from the prison gates.

Boles, alias Black Bart, disappeared after his release. He was never heard from again.

There was one report that Boles returned to holding up stagecoaches. While it was never proven, some thought it was Bart that robbed a Wells Fargo stage on November 14, 1888. The lone bandit in that holdup left a note that read:

> *"So here I've stood while wind and rain*
> *Have not the trees a sobbin'*
> *And risked my life for that damned stage*
> *That wasn't worth the robbin'.*

When carefully examined by Wells Fargo detective James B. Hume, the note was declared a hoax and not the work of Black Bart. Humes said he was sure Black Bart had permanently retired.

This declaration brought on speculation that Wells Fargo may have pensioned off Black Bart after his departure from prison on the condition that he not rob any more stages.

New York newspapers reported Black Bart died in 1917, something that was never confirmed. Before that, Detective Hume received a report that the outlaw died in the high California mountains while hunting game.

While the outlaw gained considerable fame for his stage holdups, it should be remembered, he never fired a shot.

Chapter 22

The Historic Blue Umbrella

The mysterious blue umbrella.

It was a simple blue silk umbrella, but it played a major role in getting California's official admission papers safely from Washington to San Francisco by way of Panama.

It is not the umbrella, but the story behind it that warrants notice. At the time, California was fighting to convince Congress to admit the state into the union. There was strong opposition from slave state representatives.

An event that is believed to have helped sway the approval by Congress revolves around the wife and daughter of E. C. Crosby. Crosby was a prominent participant in the affairs of San Francisco, as well a former United States Minister to Guatemala.

When Crosby came to California, his wife and daughter remained in New York, with plans to join him at a later date.

At this time, a bill to recognize California as a state was being bitterly opposed in Washington. California decided to send a delegation to Washington to shore up the state's interests.

Among the delegation was General John Bidwell. Crosby asked the general to meet his wife and daughter in New York and help arrange for their trip to California, which Bidwell readily agreed to do.

After making the travel arrangements, General Bidwell continued to Washington where he and other California delegates entered the statehood fight. One of the most prominent opponents to the bill was New York State Senator William H. Seward.

The outcome appeared bleak for California, and the Senate essentially pigeonholed the statehood bill. The delegation decided to give up the fight and return to California.

Before returning to California, however, Bidwell visited Mrs. Crosby and her daughter again, this time to tell them of the earlier departure date. Bidwell told Mrs. Crosby of Senator Seward's objection, and said California's statehood measure was not likely to pass until a new congress was convened.

This comment brought a glint into the eye of Mrs. Crosby. "You don't mean, general, that your fears for the bill center around any possible action on the part of Senator Seward?"

"Yes, madam," said the general, "and if I could be assured of the friendship of the Senator from your State, I would feel certain that our bill would be passed before the close of the present session."

Mrs. Crosby and Senator Seward had been schoolmates. They had grown up as neighbors in the same town and she felt confident that her influence might be exerted on behalf of California.

She suggested that Senator Seward be invited to her home as a guest at a farewell dinner before her departure for California. The rest is history.

Soon after the party, Senator Seward stood on the Senate floor and expressed the hope that his colleagues should admit California to the union unconditionally, and at once.

This is where the blue silk umbrella comes into the picture. Mrs. Crosby and her daughter had purchased new umbrellas for the trip to California on the advice of General Bidwell who knew of the tropical rains they would encounter.

General Bidwell decided to give the official documents related to California statehood to Mrs. Crosby. He believed the papers would be in safer keeping with her than in the hands of other members of the California delegation.

Mrs. Crosby, in turn, entrusted the papers to the care of her daughter. The papers became Miss

Crosby's personal treasure, and remained under her pillow during the trip down the Atlantic Coast.

When the travelers began the voyage of seven days and nights in an open boat along the Chagres River, where heavy rains were encountered, Miss Crosby adopted another strategy.

She sacrificed her own comfort and placed the papers in the folds of her silk umbrella, which she never opened to protect herself from the rains.

When the Californians arrived in San Francisco, they were welcomed by thousands of anxious people with news about the statehood issue. The good news brought a burst of applause from the greeters.

The documents had arrived dry and safely, tucked into the creases of Miss Crosby's new umbrella. *(This incident reported in the San Francisco Call on 31 December 1905)*

Chapter 23

California's Missions

If Spain had not established California's series of missions, Russians might have settled the territory.

King Charles III of Spain found himself in a difficult position. Spain claimed the region that is now California 200 years before the missions were established. While the land was fertile and near the sea, no Spanish settlements had been started.

There were clear rumblings that Russia was interested in the territory and California had great future potential. It was an ideal place to establish cities, but it offered something more important to Spain, safe harbors for its trading ships.

To strengthen its hold on *Alta California*, Jose Galvez, Spain's *visitador general* to the region, was ordered to establish mission settlements. He asked for the help of Father Junipero Serra to lead the project. In all, 21 missions were built in *Alta California*. The first was Mission San Diego de Alcala.

1. Mission San Diego de Alcala (1769)

The first structure Father Serra built was a crude brushwood shelter, which, on July 16, 1769, became the first church of Christ in California. At first, the Indians were slow in coming to the church for their conversion to Christianity. When they did come, it was only to steal as much as they could.

Santa Barbara---The Queen of the Missions

Eventually, Father Jayme and Father Dumetz, who were left in charge of the San Diego missionary work by Father Serra, decided to move the mission to a site six miles away. Its first site had poor farming ground, and the priests were having difficulties with soldiers in the neighboring presidio.

On November 4, 1775, a large party of Indians attacked the mission, killing Father Jayme. This forced the missionaries to return to the military base.

Eventually, the missionaries returned to the valley site.

147

In July 1776, they built a temporary church. It wasn't until the year 1813 that the church was completed in the "mission style".

At the height of its prosperity, Mission San Diego owned 20,000 sheep, 10,000 cattle, and 1,250 horses. The mission's property covered an area of 50,000 acres and gained a reputation for great wine.

2. Mission San Carlos Borromeo de Carmelo (1770)

Instead of building in Monterey, where they had first arrived, Fathers Serra and Juan Crespi decided to locate the new mission in Carmel Valley. The soil was better for growing crops there and it was located away from the Monterey Presidio and its soldiers.

This mission became Father Serra's favorite, and became the headquarters of the mission chain. Fathers Serra and Crespi were buried at the foot of the altar at this church.

3. San Antonio de Padua (1771)

Father Junipero Serra felt there was a real need for a mission at in a valley of the Santa Lucia Mountains. This mission did not start well. The river went dry and the first harvest failed. The padres could not believe that rivers full of water in the winter would be dry in the summer.

Mission San Antonio became famous for the golden palomino horses raised there. Mission San

Antonio de Padua is the only mission whose surroundings remain as they were originally.

4. Mission San Gabriel Arcangel (1771)

Father Serra wanted to close the long gap between his own San Carlos Borromeo de Carmelo mission near Monterey and the mission in San Diego. In the summer of 1771, he established two new missions, San Antonio de Padua, a day's journey to the south of Carmel, and at San Gabriel, a convenient distance north of San Diego.

The mission was relocated to its present site in 1776, and construction of its present buildings began in 1796.

5. San Luis Obispo de Tolosa (1772)

This is the fifth mission in the chain founded by Father Junipero Serra. Portola named the location "Valley of the Bears" when he and his soldiers encountered many fierce bears between the mouth of the Santa Maria River and the present site of San Luis Obispo.

Indians attacked the mission three different times setting the roof, then made of thatch, on fire. As a result, the padres developed a roof tile to protect the structures. Soon, all missions benefited from this development. Thatched roofs were replaced with tile throughout the mission chain.

6. Mission San Francisco de Asis (1776)

The site for Mission San Francisco de Asis bordered a little *laguna,* or inlet, which de Anza discovered when he explored the area earlier. The explorer named the inlet *laguna de Nuestra Senora de los Dolores.* The mission is better known today as Miss Dolores than as San Francisco de Asis.

7. Mission San Juan Capistrano (1776)

Here the padres wanted to build a church of really great proportions. Isidor Aguilar, an expert stonemason, was in charge of construction.

He incorporated features into this mission not found in others. Instead of the usual tile roof,

Aguilar designed a ceiling that was divided into six great domes.

Men, women, and children all carried stones from a creek bed four miles away for the construction. Limestone was crushed into powder to form a mortar, which was more resistant to erosion than stone.

It took nine years to construct the church. The stonemason died before the work was completed. It was finished in 1806, but demolished by an earthquake in 1812. Reconstruction of the church began in 1922.

The little church at Capistrano is the only existing structure in which Father Junipero Serra is known to have said Mass. It is also known as the site where the swallows return each year on or about March 19.

8. Mission Santa Clara de Asis (1777)

Heavy winter rains washed the walls away before Mission Santa Clara de Asis was completed. The site was moved to higher ground. Father Serra came to lay the first brick of the new building.

A ship arrived in Monterey carrying two bells for the mission. They were gifts from the King of Spain. In receiving the bells, the padre in charge said they must ring at eight-thirty each night. The mission was nearly destroyed by an earthquake in 1812.

9. Mission San Buenaventura (1782)

Mission San Buenaventura was the ninth and last mission established by Father Junipero Serra. The padres taught the Indians to dam up water and build canals. Buenaventura was sometimes called *"the place of the canals."*

10. Mission Santa Barbara (1776)

Gaspar de Portola once camped on the site where the Mission Santa Barbara is built. This mission included a military presidio. It was the first mission to be established by Father Serra's successor, Father Fermin Lasuen.

Santa Barbara, the *"Queen of the Missions"*, was the only mission to remain in constant occupation by the Franciscan Order from the day of its founding down to the present time. The rooms, which house the mission's museum, have been in uninterrupted use for more than two hundred years.

11. Mission La Purisma Concepcion (1787)

The full name of this mission at Lompoc in Santa Barbara County is La Purisma Concepcion de Maria Santisma: The Immaculate Conception of Mary the Most Pure. Father Fermin Lasuen gave the mission its name. It was the 11th mission to be founded.

Father Junipero Serra gave orders before he died that there had to be three missions in the area to take care of the Chumash tribes living there. While his wish was granted, it did not turn out as he had hoped.

Diseases of the white man hit the natives of this mission hard. Within three years, five hundred were buried because of small pox and measles.

12. Mission Santa Cruz (1791)

Mission Santa Cruz was adjacent to the site of California's first real estate development. *Branciforte.* Branciforte contributed to the downfall of Mission Santa Cruz.

Branciforte was conceived as a sort of eighteenth century welfare state, with the Spanish idea of "mixing the races". The plan, and the mission, both failed.

13. Mission Nuestra Senora de la Soledad (1791)

Spanish explorer Portola named the area Soledad after the Spanish word for "solitude". The mission was in trouble from its inception. The gifts to equip it went astray in shipment. The church, repaired in 1824, completely collapsed in 1832.

14. Mission San Jose (1797)

Mission San Jose became headquarters for the fighters of the hostile Indians who lived in the area. Destroyed by an earthquake in 1868, restoration was completed by 1985. Today, the exterior of the mission appears much as it did when completed in 1809.

15, Mission San Juan Bautista (1797)

Instead of a long narrow nave, Mission San Juan Bautista builders erected a church with three naves. When completed in 1812, it was the largest in the province and the only structure of its kind ever built by the Franciscans in California.

16. Mission San Miguel de Arcangel (1797)

The founding of Mission San Miguel completed the northern half of the mission chain from San Luis Obispo to San Francisco. In 1806, a serious fire destroyed most of the buildings.

The mission soon recovered with the help of other missions. The last Franciscan left San Miguel in 1840 and Mexican Governor Pio Pico sold the last remnants of the mission in 1846.

17. Mission San Fernando Rey de Espana (1797)

Located on the highway leading directly to Los Angeles, Mission San Fernando was a common stopping place for travelers on El Camino Real.

18. Mission San Luis Rey de Francia (1798)

San Luis Rey was referred to as "The King of the Missions". It was the largest one built in California. The mission had the most and best wine in southern California.

19. Mission Santa Ines (1804)

Mission Santa Ines was well known for its fine saddles and silver designs. The owners of the ranchos around the mission admired and wanted the saddles for their fine horses.

20. Mission San Rafael Arcangel (1817)

Mission San Rafael had problems early in its existence. Living near the mission was a strong Indian chief named Marin. He made trouble for the mission guards.

The *padre* asked the Spanish soldiers for help. Marin lost the battle, but the mission is now located in "Marin" County.

21. Mission San Francisco de Solano (1823)

Father Jose Altimira founded the last of the California missions, San Francisco de Solano. The Indians called the site *Sonoma,* or Valley of the Moon. The mission was considered an important Spanish settlement separating the Russian colony at Fort Ross from the rest of occupied California.

Secularization of the missions took them from church control. Both the mission lands and the Indians were put under civil control. The plight of the Indian worsened when the church was no longer there to provide and protect him.

While Indians were promised land and cattle, few were able to make the transition to ordinary Mexican citizen. The Indian was trapped into competing with Mexicans whose culture was rooted in centuries of experience with profit motive.

The Mexican Congress passed the Act of Secularization in 1833. By 1836, missions no longer formally existed.

Chapter 24

The Mormon Battalion

A reunion of the Mormon Battalion.

There were eight hundred covered wagons loaded with emigrants gathered on the banks of the Missouri River on July 1, 1846. Some of the emigrants walked beside their covered wagons, a few rode, and nearly three thousand pulled handcarts.

These were Mormons who were on the move again. They were driven from their homes and farms in New York and Ohio, and were now camped at

Council Bluffs, Iowa, before continuing their journey west.

While in the midst of difficulties of moving thousands of people across the wilderness of Iowa, the Latter-day Saints were asked by the United States government to provide a contingent of 500 men for the Army. The men were wanted to help fight the war against Mexico.

The Mormon Battalion would follow Colonel Stephen Watts Kearny, commander of the First Dragoons, to the west to New Mexico and California to claim those distant lands for the United States.

There were dissenters among the Mormon leaders about the logic of raising a Mormon Battalion. They remembered, painfully, the shabby treatment accorded their followers when they attempted to colonize in New York and Illinois.

Mormon leader Brigham Young quickly grasped the advantages of raising such a battalion. The Mormons needed cash to establish a new settlement. If the U.S. government wanted to pay cash for Mormon volunteers, so be it.

"If we want the privilege of going where we can worship God according to the dictates of our consciences, we must raise the Battalion," declared Young.

In a recruiting visit to the Mormon camp, U.S. Army Captain James Allen assured the volunteers they would receive pay rations and other allowances from the day they were mustered into service, the same as those in the regular army.

Five hundred Mormon volunteers signed up for 12 months service with the U.S. army. There were some who believed the calling for 500 Mormon volunteers was simply another way concocted to destroy the Saints.

The Mormon Battalion was formed to fight against the Mexicans with whom the United States was at war. Besides the men, there were 32 women, of which 20 were laundresses hired at private's pay, which left with the Battalion.

Some of the officers chose to take their families and possessions in their own wagons at no expense to the government. The Army permitted this.

The Battalion's march from the grand encampment at Council Bluffs to southern California became the longest sustained military march in U.S. history. The march began July 21, 1846 with 521 volunteers.

The military group marched 2,000 miles from Fort Leavenworth, Kansas, by way of Santa Fe, New Mexico, to San Diego, arriving there January 1847. There the Mormon Battalion served on garrison duty.

The Mormon Battalion blazed a route across the desert southwest that would be followed for the next century and more. Their route became used as the Southern Overland Trail, and is today the approximate rout of Interstate 8 between Yuma and San Diego.

When General Winfield Scott and his 10,000-man army seized and held Mexico City, and peace was ratified, the men in the Mormon Battalion were discharged and allowed to rejoin their families.

Chapter 25

Railroads Ruled the State

An early Southern Pacific passenger train.

It was no secret that "Big Business" was in charge of California's government.

Machine politics was the order of the day. At the forefront was the powerful Southern Pacific Railroad, which wanted to maintain its monopoly over rates and services.

The Big Four dominated California. The Big Four included California's most illustrious business giants. These were Leland Stanford, Collis P. Huntington, Charles Crocker, and Mark Hopkins. Building the Central and Southern Pacific railroads made the four associates wealthy and powerful.

Clockwise from top left, Leland Stanford, Colis P. Huntington, Charles Crocker, and Mark Hopkins comprised the Big Four.

The railroad's lobbyist, William F. Herrin of San Francisco, saw to it that a weekend roundtrip ticket

164

to San Francisco was left on the desk of every legislator.

Newspaper editors were subsidized with monthly payments to obtain favorable publicity. California was a state where a kind word for railroads was a rarity. Railroads were so powerful in California that they comprised a government within a government.

Collis P. Huntington, one of the big four who established Southern Pacific, had amassed a fortune of $70,000,000, and owned enough trackage to connect the North and South Poles. He could travel from Newport News, Virginia, to San Francisco without ever riding on anyone else's rails.

By the end of the 1870s, the Big Four monopolized California transportation. They controlled 2,340 miles of railroad tracks, including 85 percent of the railroad lines in the state.

Southern Pacific Railroad owned newspapers, huge tracts of land, and all transportation facilities. Southern Pacific was the state's biggest landowner and its biggest employer of labor.

The railroads helped those who had property and influence more than it did those striving to succeed. They were a boon to those well situated on the new transit lines, but the railroads undermined those not so fortunately placed.

Railroads did encourage economic growth. One of the first results of the advent of the railroad was phenomenal urbanization. A prime example of this was Oakland, which was a steamship port settled in 1850.

The Big Four located Central Pacific's terminal at Oakland. The fact that Leland Stanford, one of the Big Four, held a substantial interest in Oakland's Waterfront Company undoubtedly played a major role in that decision.

The trains had an immediate effect on Oakland. Commuters and travelers jammed Oakland's shops, hotels, and restaurants. Oakland's progress was typical of other railroad towns in California.

Central/Southern Pacific Railroad maintained a monopoly in California that allowed it to impose high freight tariffs on farmers, often pricing them out of the national market.

Railroad rates were arbitrary. It wasn't unusual for railroad agents to demand an agricultural shipper open his books to an agent before a shipping rate was set. This rate was generally set at the highest rate the agent believed the shipper could pay.

No railroad in any other region in the nation enjoyed the freedom from competition, as did the Central/Southern Pacific. They favored big shippers with rebates at the expense of small farmers and other shippers. The railroad used its broad powers to adopt any system of freight rates the traffic would bear.

The farmers fought back by forming their own organization, the Grange in 1867. Under Granger guidance, farmers created cooperative facilities that would bypass middleman merchants as well as railroads.

During the 1870s, the Grange influenced several states to pass laws controlling railroad practices. Federal courts consistently struck down these same laws.

Transportation competition came when Santa Fe Railroad entered Los Angeles from the Midwest in the mid 1880s and engaged Southern Pacific in a rate war that helped to ignite a real estate boom.

Santa Fe later brought an independent rail line up the San Joaquin Valley and built a connection to San Francisco Bay at Richmond. Later, in the 1900s, both Union Pacific and Western Pacific completed their own lines from California to the east.

Even so, the Southern Pacific continued to control the most important tracks in all the major markets.

In 1878 a clamor arose calling for a convention to revise California's 1849 constitution. Regulation of railroads and other corporations consumed the most energy of the proponents of constitutional change.

The new constitution produced by the convention was so detailed and complex that it satisfied almost no one. It narrowly passed only because of its promises to make railroad rates more equitable.

Even with its shortcomings, the new constitution established important principles of state economic regulation, including supervision of public utilities, such as railroads.

167

Chapter 26

California and Slavery

Slavery was never an issue for California voters. A ban on slavery was clearly stated in California's first constitution drafted in 1849.

Despite the constitutional ban on slavery, it did not clear up the legal status of blacks in California during the Gold Rush.

Blacks could neither vote nor testify in court cases involving whites. Blacks in California remained neither slave nor citizen until the Civil War.

Consider the case of Archy Lee, a Mississippi slave who arrived in Sacramento with his master in 1857. After one year in the area, the master decided to return to the South.

Lee did not want to go. He claimed that under the laws and constitution of California, he was a free man and could not be forced back into slavery. Lee received assistance from white attorneys and was backed up by other blacks in the community.

When the case appeared in Court, Lee won. The court ruled that upon accepting employment in California, Lee's master became a resident subject to its laws and, therefore, could not own a slave.

The master appealed the decision to the state supreme court. That body confirmed the lower court's decision, but then reached a peculiar and inconsistent conclusion.

Because the slave master was "young and inexperienced" with the law, the court held the first decision should be overturned and Lee be returned to slavery.

A federal commissioner ultimately reversed the state supreme court's ruling on grounds that Lee had broken no law, state or federal, and should be free.

Lee wasted little time in exercising his freedom. He, along with many other black Californians, left for the Fraser River mines in British Columbia where the legal climate surrounding slavery was more predictable.

Fugitive slave fights continued in California. In San Jose, in 1850, a street brawl involved a white man beating a Negro with a club. The town's marshal took both men into custody.

In court, the white man insisted the Negro was his slave. He claimed the Negro's association with free Negroes in San Jose had made the slave disobedient and that he would not leave the city with his master.

Friendly authorities spirited the Negro away in time to avoid a writ presented too late to the *alcalde.*

In Sacramento, a few months after the San Jose case, another street brawl occurred, involving a black fugitive slave named Charles. The judge set the Negro free, pointing out to the man who claimed to be Charles' master that California laws made the Negro a free man.

170

Still another slave case occurred in San Francisco in March 1851. A Missourian brought to the mines what newspapers described as a "yellow boy" named Frank who decided to run away. His master tracked him down and had him confined preparatory to returning to Missouri.

In San Francisco, S. W. Holladay, a legal aid attorney, presented a writ to Judge Morrison to set the Negro Free. Judge Morrison ruled that Frank did not come to California as a fugitive and that his running away within the boundaries of the state was not offenses against California law.

During interrogation, Frank stated that he had been a slave in Missouri. In a twist of irony, the judge rejected this bit of testimony, contending that California law made Negro testimony illegal in civil and criminal cases.

A champion for slave owners emerged in 1852 in the form of Assemblyman Henry A. Crabb, a southern aristocrat. Crabb introduced The Fugitive Slave Act that gave white men arbitrary powers in returning Negroes whom they claimed as slaves in southern states.

Senator David Broderick strongly opposed the bill without success. Broderick claimed a callously capricious former owner with the talents of a Negro kidnapper would abuse the measure. It passed fourteen to nine with Broderick in the minority.

Broderick's fears were soon realized the following year when a former slave owner attempted to return a free Negro girl in Auburn to slavery. Fortunately for the girl, a local lawyer held the young woman's

171

freedom papers, which he produced, in court. The claimant in this case was the son of the man who freed the girl, and who later claimed not to know of his father's action.

In the mining town of Gold Springs in Tuolumne County, Stephen Hill, a Negro, had been free long enough to accumulate property valued at $4,000. Men claiming to be agents of his former owner imprisoned him.

In addition, the men were able to destroy Hill's freedom papers. Hill was taken to Stockton where a daring escape was managed, apparently by the collusion of sympathetic Caucasians

In 1855, California Negroes marshaled their forces with a meeting of the First Colored Convention. The main concern was the testimony of Negroes in civil and criminal cases where white men were involved.

The denial of this right was a tragic handicap to the Negro whose wife or daughter had been raped by a white man without white witnesses. Likewise, the Negro who was robbed in open daylight in his shop was defenseless unless there were white witnesses.

Some reports claim Negro farmers were ejected from their farms because they were not allowed to testify about their ownership.

It wasn't until 1863 that the state legislature revised the testimony laws and the Negro was finally allowed to testify in court. By the time of the Fourth Colored Convention in 1865, Negro leadership was turning itself to the other problems, including education and suffrage.

Chapter 27

Saving the Wilderness

John Muir said humanity was selfish and arrogant in assuming that all nature had been created for its sole benefit,. With its machines that tore up the earth and disordered nature, Muir claimed "Lord Man" had usurped the power of God to determine which species lived or died.

President Teddy Roosevelt and John Muir in Yosemite.

Muir was California's and America's champion of nature and conservation. He wrote the following in a vain try to prevent the damning of Hetch-Hetchy Valley on the Mokulumne River.

"It is impossible to overestimate the value of wild mountains and mountain temples. They are the greatest of our natural resources, God's best gifts, but none, however high and holy, is beyond reach of the spoiler."

It was in part through Muir's efforts that Congress created Yosemite National Park. He was instrumental in the creation of Sequoia, Mount Ranier, Petrified Forest and Grand Canyon national parks. He was often referred to as the "Father of Our National Park System."

Muir was a friend of President Theodore Roosevelt and one of the founders of the Sierra Club, and served as the organization's president until his death in 1914.

Theodore Roosevelt wrote, "I was interested and a little surprised to find that John Muir cared little for birds or bird songs, and knew little about them. The hermit thrushes meant nothing to him, the trees and the flowers and the cliffs were everything."

In the 1870s, author Mark Stoll wrote, "Muir realized that the pure wilderness areas of America were fast disappearing before the woodsman's axe, the shepherd's flock, and the miner's pick."

Muir was born on April 21, 1838, in Dunbar, Scotland. The Muir family immigrated to the United States in 1849, settling in Wisconsin. His father was harsh in his discipline and worked his family from dawn to dusk.

In Muir's youth, his father forbade him to study anything but the Bible, believing that to pursue other forms of knowledge was to sin against God.

While Muir traveled the world, it was California's Sierra Nevada and Yosemite that most captivated him. He was fascinated that the landscape showed no signs of civilization.

Muir saw nature as not just a storehouse of raw material for man's economic needs, but as a spiritual resource as well. Showing remarkable insight, he wrote, "When we try to pick out anything in itself, we find it hitched to everything else in the universe."

While he fought hard against decimation of nature, he wasn't always successful. One battle he lost was his fight against the damming of Hetch-Hetchy Valley to provide a water reservoir to supply San Francisco.

While the battle was lost, it did inspire conservationists to work tirelessly to prevent dams in other national parks, such as the Grand Canyon and Dinosaur National Monument.

In writing about man's place in the universe, Muir asked, "Why should man value himself as more than a small part of the one great unit of creation? The universe would be incomplete without man, but it would also be incomplete without the smallest transmicroscopic creature that dwells beyond our conceitful eyes and knowledge."

He added, "From the dust of the earth, from the common elementary fund, the Creator has made Homo sapiens. From the same material he has made every other creature, however noxious and insignificant to us. They are earth-born companions and our fellow mortals."

Muir died in a Los Angeles hospital in 1914 after a short illness. He was 76 years old. The importance of Muir is easily documented by the fact that all of his many books are still in print.

April 21, John Muir's birth date, has been designated as John Muir Day in California.

Chapter 28

The Japanese Internment

December 7, 1941, the Japanese attacked Pearl Harbor. This act brought the wrath of Americans across the U.S. down on the Japanese immigrants.

Even before that dreadful day, the Japanese had been the subject of derision in California. From the time the Japanese first arrived in California, they were subjected to the same hostility and discrimination that the Chinese had suffered before them.

During the 1880s, Asian immigrants to the U.S. were primarily Chinese. Between 1890 and 1900, less than one thousand Japanese immigrants came into the United States each year.

The number suddenly jumped to more than 12,000. In 1910, an estimated 41,000 Japanese were living in the United States and this number doubled during the next 10 years.

The U.S. banned further immigration from Japan in 1924 and the Japanese who had entered the country earlier were barred from becoming U.S. citizens.

Many Californians looked upon the Japanese as a greater menace than the Chinese. They were more ambitious and self-assertive than the Chinese *coolie* immigrants.

Japanese immigrants were not content to remain farm laborers. Instead, they obtained land, often marginal tracts bought or leased from large growers. They became successful truck farmers, raising tomatoes, vegetables, and a variety of fresh produce.

By 1910, Japanese farmers owned an estimated 17,000 acres in California, leased another 80,000 acres, and sharecropped still another 60,000 acres.

In 1913, the California legislature passed the Alien Land Law, prohibiting foreigners not eligible for citizenship from purchasing farmland, or leasing such holdings for longer than three years.

As a result, the Japanese developed their own subculture. By applying the labor-intensive methods they had used in their homeland, the Japanese became dominant in California agriculture.

The Alien Land Law was full of loopholes and the Japanese continued to increase their control over fruit, vegetable, and other valuable farmland. Ownership was put into the names of their American-born children, who were citizens because of their U.S. birth, for instance.

When the Japanese bombed Pearl Harbor, Hawaii, instant fear spread across California and the U.S.

That very afternoon, the Department of Defense and the FBI began detaining Japanese residents in the United States who were suspected of being subversives. By the end of the day, 737 Japanese and Americans of Japanese descent in California were arrested.

179

Scary reports kept emerging. One, which proved false, was that 20,000 Japanese in the San Francisco area were ready for organized action. Another report claimed a Japanese submarine had been sighted off California's coast.

These and other reports fueled the atmosphere, calling for action against the Japanese. To the American citizenry, all Japanese were suspect and should be incarcerated.

All residents of Japanese descent were ordered to surrender cameras, short-wave radios, binoculars, shotguns, and other materials usable for spying or sabotage.

Finally, the order for evacuation came on May 3, 1942. The order stated that all Japanese, both alien and non-alien, were to be evacuated to internment camps by 12 o'clock noon on May 9, 1942.

In one case, F.B.I. agents swooped down on a Los Angeles baseball field. They apprehended the players on one team called the Los Angeles Nippons. The F.B.I. had been compiling lists of "potentially dangerous" Japanese Americans since 1932. Most were merely teachers, businessmen or journalists.

America was at war and precautions were necessary. The U.S. officially entered World War II on December 8, 1941, the day following the Japanese bombing of Pearl Harbor, Hawaii.

There was rabid anti-Japanese racism surfacing throughout California. California Governor Culbert Olson and then California Attorney General Earl Warren wanted the Japanese contained to better monitor their activities. Warren was later to become Chief Justice of the U.S. Supreme Court.

The wholesale uprooting of Japanese and placing them in internment camps was one of the most shameful acts committed by the U.S. government during the 20th century.

Many Japanese-Americans asked to serve the U.S. in the military, volunteering to fight against the Japanese soldiers. They simply wanted a chance to prove their loyalty to the U.S. Thousands were able to do exactly that.

In Hawaii, thousands of Japanese-Americans volunteered for the Military Intelligence Service or to serve in the segregated Japanese-American 100th Battalion of the U.S. Army.

Another army unit was the 442nd Regimental Team. This Japanese-American unit was the most decorated for its size and length of service in American military history.

Many of the Japanese in California at that time would have been U.S. citizens except law forbade them to do so. A U.S. law passed in 1924 had virtually forbidden Japanese immigration and extension of American citizenship. For this reason, most of the arrested suspects were classified as "enemy aliens".

Many of the Japanese were evacuated to racetracks, such as Santa Anita and Tanforan, or to fairgrounds. Others were moved to less hospitable areas such as Manzanar Camp east of the Sierra Nevada in the high desert region of the Owens Valley.

It was nearly 50 years after the internment of approximately 120,000 Japanese that the U.S. apologized for this injustice and the Civil Liberties Act of 1988 was signed into law.

The Act authorized payments of $20,000 to each person who suffered as a result of the internment.

Chapter 29

Russia Wanted California

The establishment of the Russian Colony at Fort Ross in the Sonoma region demonstrated the weakness of Spain who had kept California closed to foreign settlement.

Before the Russians arrived aboard their large sailing ship in March 1812 in Bodega Bay, San Francisco Bay marked the northern limit of Spanish settlement.

Russia's interest in the area came when Count Nikolai Rezanov sailed to San Francisco seeking supplies for their scurvy-ridden outpost in Sitka, Alaska. While in San Francisco, Rezanov met the family of Don Jose Arguello, *commandante* of the port.

Rezanov and Concepcion Arguello, the 16-year old daughter of the commandante, fell in love and became engaged. It was this relationship that allowed Rezanov to secure the supplies he sought, as Spain forbade trading with foreigners at that time.

History tells us that Rezanov died on his return trip to Russia, and it was years before the faithful Concepcion learned why he had not returned to her.

Even so, Rezanov's reports to his Russian superiors, spurred the Russians to establish a base for shipping food and other supplies to its Alaskan fur trading posts, as well as for hunting sea otter along California's coast.

The site the Russians desired was the location of a Kashaya Indian Village. One account claims the Russians acquired the site for "three blankets, three pairs of breeches, two axes, three hoes, and some beads."

There the Russians built Fort Ross. The name "Ross" is believed to be a shortened version of "Rossiya," the Russia of Tsarist days.

The site of Fort Ross offered the Russians a harbor, plentiful water, good forage, and a nearby supply of wood with which to build the fort. The site was located on a bluff above a stream now known as the Russian River. The Fort was officially dedicated on August 13, 1812.

Life at the Russian colony centered on the hunting of sea otters. The sea otter pelts were worth one hundred dollars in the China trade.

The Russians used Alaskans from Kodiak to hunt the sea otters. The Alaskans and their Russian overseers ranged the coast from Baja California to Oregon in search of marine mammals.

By 1820, the extensive hunting of sea otters depleted otter population. Agriculture and livestock then became the primary activity for those occupying Fort Ross.

Several factors prevented the Russian foothold in California from prospering. The moist air caused rust disease in their wheat crops and their harvest was never enough to supply their Alaskan trading posts.

The Russians made an agreement with the Hudson Bay Company in Oregon to acquire supplies for the Alaska posts. The Russians became convinced, too, that the United States would absorb California.

The structures at Fort Ross were built of redwood, using joinery techniques that were typical of maritime carpentry. A wooden palisade surrounded the site. There were two blockhouses, one on the north corner and one on the south, complete with cannons that could command the entire area.

The Russian-American Company flag, with its double-headed eagle, flew over the stockade.

The Russians tried to sell Fort Ross to the Mexican government. Failing in that attempt, they approached John A. Sutter, builder of Sutter's Fort in Sacramento.

Sutter sent his trusted assistant, John Bidwell, to Fort Ross to gather up the arms, ammunition, hardware, and other valuables, including the livestock and bring them to Sacramento.

The buildings that were not dismantled by Sutter were used by a number of successive owners. In 1873, George W. Call, who established the 15,000-acre Call Ranch, acquired it.

There were other foreigners who made their way to California before 1820. Among them was John Gilroy, a Scottish sailor on an English ship that arrived in Monterey in 1812. Because of illness, Gilroy got off the vessel.

Gilroy was later baptized and naturalized, and married the daughter of Ignacio Ortega. He then became a ranchero. The town of Gilroy, south of San Jose, bears his name.

185

As for Concepcion Arguello, who waited patiently for the return of Count Nikolai Rezanov, she eventually became a nun in her attempt to escape the memories of her beloved.

Chapter 30

How Dogtown Got Its Name

The story of how Dogtown got its name dates back to the early Gold Rush days. Dogtown was established as a gold mining camp.

There were only 10 houses, but 16 dogs in town. The origin of the dogs goes back to the arrival of a Mrs. Bassett, who had traveled on foot on what is now the Oroville-Susanville highway.

According to various historic accounts, Mrs. Bassett had neither horse nor wagon among her possessions when she arrived at the tiny camp overlooking the West Branch of the Feather River Canyon. She did, however, own three dogs of uncertain ancestry, one male and two females.

Mrs. Bassett tried her luck at gold panning without much success. Her luck brightened, however, with the birth of several puppies soon after her arrival.

The early miners in California were often a homesick lot, having neither family nor companions. The perceptive Mrs. Bassett began selling her puppies to the lonesome local miners for one large pinch of gold dust each.

Soon, every cabin and tent in the area had a canine companion. Not only miners, but storeowners, saloonkeepers and other residents of the area soon had a dog or two.

There is little wonder that strangers in the area would remark, "This must be Dogtown!"

The name stuck. (The "Dogtown" in Butte County is not to be confused with a "Dogtown" in Mono County.)

Until 1859, Dogtown was not widely known nor highly populated, something that the local residents preferred. The community gained wide fame soon after, however, when a 54-pound gold nugget was found on the slopes of Sawmill Peak.

A.K. Stearns, a workman, found the gold nugget in the Willard Claim, a hydraulic mine owned by three miners, Willard, Wetherbee, and Smith. The nugget was later valued at $10,690. At today's prices, estimates put the value of the nugget at more than $350,000. Reports claim a 96-ounce nugget was found on the same site in 1854.

This rich piece of ore was dubbed the "Dogtown Nugget" and made the headlines of newspapers across the United States. The news started a small gold rush of its own to the Dogtown area.

The women in Dogtown didn't appreciate their town's name. They resented having to write "Dogtown" on their letters to family and friends back home. It should be noted that it cost two dollars for postage to send a letter from Marysville to Magalia and took up to three weeks for delivery.

On August 16, 1860, The *Marysville Appeal* ran a letter from one of the discontented wives living in Dogtown.

"We should hate to live in a place called 'Dogtown', particularly if we had a large correspondence and had to write the name frequently."

The women of Dogtown waged a strong campaign to change the name. After much discussion, Dogtown was renamed "Magalia", the Latin word for "cottages". The Magalia name was apparently adopted for the Magalia mine that was discovered in the area in 1855.

Large-scale mining continued in Dogtown or Magalia until the 1890s.

Chapter 31

What's A Clamper?

The Ancient and Honorable Order of E Clampus Vitus was founded back in the gold rush days. As with all its irreverent behavior, Clampers never put a period after the E in their name.

Pinning down the history and true purpose of these *"Clampers"* is about as difficult as lassoing a snake. Even more difficult to believe is that this organization that began as a spoof on other lodges and secret societies still exists with a rousing membership across the country.

As one Clamper historian wrote, "The early meetings of E Clampus Vitus were devoted so completely to drinking and carousing that none of the Clampers was ever in any condition to keep minutes, let alone remember what had happened the next day!"

The Clampers claimed that all their members were officers and "of equal indignity", but that some, such as the Clampatriarch and the Noble Grand Humbug, were more equal than others were.

According to tradition, a person could join E Clampus Vitus by invitation only and then was expected to endure an elaborate and grueling initiation ceremony. Sometimes the new initiate was blindfolded and seated on a cold wet sponge at the bottom of a wheelbarrow.

While thus positioned, one of the brothers would take the initiate for a ride "on the rock road to Dublin" over the rungs of a ladder laid on the floor.

Membership in E Clampus Vitus declined in the late 1800s, but experienced a revival in the 1930s and is even stronger today. Members typically dress up in garb, usually a red miner's shirt, a black hat, and Levi's. They still hold their outrageous initiation ceremonies.

Carl Wheat, one of the founders of the revived Order of E Clampus Vitus, described the group as the "comic strip on the page of California history."

Some accounts credit a Joe Zumwalt, of Illinois, or Missouri, depending on which account you're reading, with bringing the Clamper organization to California. Zumwalt and a Clamper brother, W. C. (or maybe C. W.) Wright were unsuccessful in opening a chapter in Hangtown (now Placerville).

After the first Chapter meeting at Mokelumne Hill in September 1851, Chapters began to spread throughout the gold country.

Drummers (traveling salesmen) often found it difficult to sell their wares unless they were Brothers in ECV. An early credo was "Clampers only patronize Brother Clampers."

Soon, many fraternal organizations, such as the Masons, Elks, and Oddfellows became prominent in the diggins'. These groups were often clannish and took their pomp and ceremony seriously.

The irreverent Clampers began cutting tin can lids into odd shapes and pinning them to their vests, mocking the fancy sashes and bejeweled vests worn by the Masons, Elks, and Oddfellows.

Life in the diggins' was hard and entertainment virtually non-existent. Brothers of E Clampus Vitus attempted to "lighten the load". They looked on the absurdity of life as a cherished commodity.

With tongues set firmly in cheek, they hailed each other as "Noble Grand Humbug," "Roisterous Iscutis," "Grand Imperturbable Hangman," "Clamps Vitus," and "Royal Gyascutis."

The group was a benevolent organization. Whenever a miner fell ill or died, the Clampers would collect food, money and other items for the widow.

Currently there are 40-some land-based chapters in California, Nevada, Utah and Arizona. There is as well the Floating Whang chapter, based offshore, and several outposts (incipient chapters) in Oregon and Colorado. The newest chapter arrival is CyberWhang Chapter, based in cyberspace. (Check the Internet).

ECV's "serious" side consists of finding, researching, and dedicating plaques to sites, incidents, and people in western history that might otherwise be overlooked. The Clampers the largest organization devoted to preserving western and mining history.

After their dedications, they traditionally have a party, known as a "doin's." This type of partying has given the Clampers a reputation as a "historical drinking society" or more correctly, "a drinking historical society".

Although they do not deny that copious amounts of "fermented, distilled, and fortified beverages" are occasionally consumed at a doin's, the group is strongly opposed to public displays of intoxication. The Clampers insist that members who imbibe have "a Brother of Sobriety holding the reins" on the ride home.

The prime requisites to becoming a Clamper are a sense of humor, an interest in western history, an open mind, and a cast iron stomach. If a man has these qualities, and strikes up a friendship with a Clamper or two, he may find himself taken into the Ancient and Honorable Order.

But one can't simply walk up to a Clamper ask, "Can I be a Clamper?" It is for the Brethren of ECV to invite prospective members to join. And if a man is asked, he should know that the invitation is only given once.

If the invitation is refused, it is never tendered again. As the Brethren of E Clampus Vitus maintain, Clampers are not made, they're born. Like gold, they just have to be discovered.

Chapter 32

Miners Ravage the Soil

It is estimated that hydraulic mining washed away six to eight times as much earth as was moved to build the Panama Canal.

From the Gold Rush of 1849 through the 1960's, California produced about 3,300 tons of gold. This is estimated at one-third of all U.S. gold production.

By 1850, there was little gold left in the mountain streams. Miners began to prospect on mountainsides above the streams. Because it was difficult to move the dirt from their diggings to water, the miners devised methods of bringing water to the diggings.

They built dams high in the mountains, and carried the water from the dams to the mining operations below through wooden flumes that were up to 45 miles long.

From the flumes, water was forced through canvas hoses and nozzles, called monitors. Under the high pressure, miners would aim the monitors at the hillsides and wash the gravel into sluices. Eventually high-pressure nozzles were devised to make them even more powerful.

Debris from hydraulic mining began to bury camps along the Yuba River with up to 200 feet of silt. There was so much sediment in the Yuba River that the riverbed rose above the level of the town of Marysville, resulting in many floods.

The grain ships between Marysville and Sacramento were unable to traverse the river. Farmlands along both the Yuba and Bear rivers were destroyed with silt from the hydraulic mining.

The force of these monitors was so great it could toss a fifty-pound rock like a cannonball or even kill a person. The monitors could wash fifty thousand tons of dirt and gravel in a day and used sixteen million gallons of water in a year.

So many conflicts arose between the "flatlanders" and the mountain miners that a judge issued a decision that literally stopped hydraulic mining. This was *The Sawyer Decision*, issued January 23, 1884. In this case, Judge Lorenzo Sawyer declared hydraulic mining illegal.

Hydraulic mining

Little plant life grows on some of these hillsides. One recent visitor to such a site remarked, "Nature here reminds one of a princess fallen into the hands of robbers who cut off her fingers for the jewels she wears."

It was not only hydraulic mining that caused problems for the environment. Mercury, used in early-day mining operations to separate gold from other materials is being found in areas of the "gold country".

While hydraulic mining used only one to two percent as much mercury as placer mining did, it created another chemical problem. It has been found that some of the tailing piles at these hydraulic mines contain elevated levels of arsenic.

The Gold Rush was a romantic era of California's rich history, but it did indeed cause damage that may last for centuries.

Chapter 33

Those Everlasting Levi's

Levi Strauss

Levi's are the only garment created in the 19th century that is still worn today.

Young Loeb Strauss emigrated from Bavaria to New York in 1847 to join and learn the dry goods business from his brothers who had a store in the city.

For a while Loeb tramped through the hills of Kentucky carrying packs loaded with thread, scissors, yarns, combs, buttons and bolts of fabric.

He was quickly attracted by news of California's Gold Rush and decided to head for San Francisco. He changed his name to Levi and became a naturalized citizen. His purpose was not to prospect for gold, but to sell supplies to the throngs of miners.

Levi opened a dry goods store in San Francisco. When he arrived in California, he had bolts of duck canvas to sell to miners as material for tents and wagon covers.

He soon became aware that the miners did not need tents and wagon covers. What they really needed was trousers.

Levi started stitching trousers from the canvas rolls he had carried to California. The trousers were readily received by the hard-working miners, and before long, it was common to hear the miners calling them, "those pants of Levi's."

As his trouser business prospered, Levi enlarged his business from a dry goods dealer to a trouser maker. In the process, he switched from canvas to stronger and softer material, cotton denim.

It was in 1872 when Strauss received a letter from Jacob Davis, a Reno, Nevada tailor. Davis was a good customer of Strauss', buying bolts of cloth for his tailoring business.

A customer of Davis, an Alkali Ike of the Comstock Mines, complained that *Levi Strauss* the pockets ripped out when he put ore in them. Davis decided to rivet them.

200

In the letter, Davis described the method he used of making pants by placing metal rivets at points of strain on the pocket corners, and at the base of the button fly.

Davis didn't have the money to patent the process. He suggested that Levi pay for the paperwork and that they get the patent together.

Levi was enthusiastic about the idea and readily agreed. The two received a patent for the process May 20, 1873.

Realizing that the riveted trousers would be popular, Levi brought Davis to San Francisco to oversee Levi Strauss' first West Coast manufacturing facility. Davis supervised the cutting of material and its delivery to individual seamstresses who worked out of their homes.

The demand for riveted "waist overalls" simply outgrew the system. Levi opened factories on Fremont and Market Streets.

Levi's brother Louis, his brother-in-law David Stern, and his nephew Nathan all joined him in the San Francisco firm.

As Levi prospered, he became active in his community. He was one of the original stockholders in the Nevada Bank of San Francisco, which eventually became Wells, Fargo Bank.

Chapter 34

The Lady Gambler

When she stepped down from the stage in Nevada City in 1854, all heads, both men and women, turned in her direction.

She appeared to be in her early twenties and her activities mystified residents of the mining town for days. She was neatly and stylishly dressed, and looked fresh even after her grueling stage ride.

Miners cast admiring glances at this classy-appearing lady. They couldn't figure out what a young woman like her would be doing in a rough and tumble town like Nevada City.

Some surmised the lady might be the town's new schoolteacher. Others thought she came to join a fiancée. Others thought even worse, that she might be a madam, or looking for such a person for whom to work.

Two young miners readily agreed to carry her bags into Fepp's Hotel where she registered as "Eleanora Dumont".

For days the elegant Madame Eleanora Dumont wandered up and down dusty Broad Street, the main street in Nevada City, peering into windows of shops that had gone out of business. Her activity only increased the curiosity of the miners as well as that of the few wives of miners living in the mining town.

Commented one woman, "There's got to be some bad in a girl with all her charms who seems to have nothing to do but strut up and down Main Street."

Finally, the mystery of Eleanor Dumont came out in the open. It happened when she handed a printing order to Editor Wait of the *Nevada Journal.*

"I want this handbill printed and distributed to every man in this town to let them know I am opening the best gambling emporium in northern California," she told the editor.

Soon after, the charming Eleanor opened "Vingt-et-Un" (French for twenty-one). It was a finely furnished and carpeted gambling saloon for only well-behaved and well-groomed men.

Madame Dumont served champagne instead of whiskey, and she dealt the cards herself. It didn't take her miner clientele long to observe that Miss Dumont knew her gambling profession well.

The smitten miners lost their hard-earned gold pokes earned from their day in the mines to the deft-fingered Miss Dumont. She seldom lost her deals or her demure smile as she collected the miner's gold. They seemed to think it a privilege just to be in her presence.

Unsatisfied with her club's limited gaming, Eleanor expanded her casino to include faro and chuck-a-luck. She hired more dealers and added a small band of violinists to entertain the gamblers.

As far as anyone knew, Eleanor Dumont had no lovers. She kept her personal life private.

It was during her second year in Nevada City that close observers saw the unflattering growth of hair on her upper lip. Because of this, she was given the equally unflattering name, *"Madame Moustache"*. Soon, it seemed, miners came to see the mustachioed lady as much as they did to gamble.

In time, Eleanor sold her Nevada City gambling emporium and began wandering through the gold country. She drifted throughout the mining camps of the western territories, even spending time in Deadwood, South Dakota, and in mining camps in Montana, Idaho and Nevada.

Eleanor Dumont became notorious throughout the west. One story tells about her being accosted by two drunks as she walked home one dark night.

"We'll take your purse," one growled.

"No, you'll not," she calmly informed the pair.

One of the robbers held a gun on her, telling her she had better hand over her purse, or else. She reached under her skirt as if to pull out her purse, but instead brought out a derringer.

Firing point blank, she killed one man and the other disappeared into the night.

Natural aging eventually replaced the youthful charms of Eleanor Dumont. She put on weight and her once hourglass figure turned plump.

Even worse, her moustache turned even more prominent, darkening her upper lip. Her gambling skill had left her and she soon turned to prostitution. She maintained a *"bawdie"* house in Bannock, Montana, at one time.

Some say that one of her girls in that enterprise was Martha Jane Canary, later known as *"Calamity*

Jane." Eleanor then moved on to San Francisco to try her luck, but that venture failed.

At one point, she gave up her fast-paced gambling and prostitution ways and settled down on a ranch in eastern Nevada. She married a small-time gambler and made the mistake of turning over her savings to him. He squandered her money and disappeared.

The once-beautiful Eleanor Dumont eventually showed up in Bodie, the "toughest town in the west." She struggled to survive and soon became an object of pity by the townspeople.

On September 13, 1879, the Aurora, Nevada, *Esmeralda Herald* carried an obituary, noting that the body of a woman was found two miles south of Bodie and was identified as that of Eleanor Dumont, more familiarly known as *"Madame Moustache."*

The gamblers and bartenders who had known Eleanor saw to it that she had a decent burial in a good cemetery, rather than in a pauper's grave.

Chapter 35

Snowshoe Thompson

Snowshoe Thompson kept snow-bound miners in the Sierra Nevada mining camps in touch with their relatives and with the outside world.

Thompson was the only man to carry the mail between the eastern foothill mining communities of California from 1856 and 1876, the year he died.

Jon Torsteinson-Rue (later changed to John A. Thompson) came to America at the age of 10 from Norway. When John was 24 years old, gold fever struck.

He tried his luck at gold mining without success. He tried ranching and it, too, held little allure, although he maintained his homestead near Placerville.

One day, Thompson read an ad in the *Sacramento Union*: "People Lost to the World; Uncle Sam needs a Mail Carrier." A carrier was needed to pick up mail at Placerville and deliver it to Genoa, Nevada, a Mormon settlement on the eastern edge of the Sierras.

His Norwegian upbringing sprang to life. John grabbed an ax, chopped down an oak, and fashioned a set of cumbersome ski-shaped snowshoes, each weighing more than 12 pounds. Such snowshoes were as common in the Telemark region of Norway as ordinary shoes.

The 10-foot staves which Thompson called "snowshoes" were actually skis. Attempts by postmen to cross the Sierra on woven Canadian and Native American snowshoes had failed until Thompson carved out his version of snowshoes.

Before applying for the mail carrier job, Thompson traveled to Placerville and practiced maneuvering over the snow until he felt ready to carry the mail. The postmaster was skeptical. He took one look at Thompson's proposed mail-carrying equipment and shook his head.

"Even men with mule teams fail to make the trip over the Sierra in the dead of winter," the postmaster warned, adding, "We found some frozen to death."

The postmaster was faced with a perplexing problem. Nobody else wanted the job, and John Thompson did. He was therefore hired.

Before his first run, gamblers wagered that Thompson would never again be seen alive. Wearing only a jacket for warmth and carrying a handful of jerked beef and a few dried biscuits, Thompson set off. He carried no water, depending on snow and icy streams along the way for liquid.

It took five days to make the 90-mile trip to Genoa and back, three to get there and two to get back. The mail route required him to ski through all kinds of conditions, and he figured it was necessary to cover 25 to 40 miles a day to keep his mail delivery on schedule.

Thompson was quickly dubbed with the nickname "Snowshoe". Two to four times a month for twenty winters, Snowshoe Thompson traveled from

Placerville to Genoa with his mail pouch, which weighed as much as 100 pounds.

People in Genoa became accustomed to Thompson's arrival time. Everyone ran outdoors to watch the tall blond Norseman descend from Genoa Peak with his bag of mail.

Even during the trips he made through driving snowstorms, Thompson said he never became lost. "I was never lost, I can't be lost," he told one reporter. "Something here in my head keeps me right."

While he never suffered from cold or frostbite, Thompson did save others who were caught in the raging snowstorms. He once found a man who had been wandering for four days in Lake Valley, completely lost.

Another time, he found James Sisson, who was lying inside a deserted cabin, his boots frozen to his feet. For 12 days, Sisson subsisted on raw flour. Thompson made Sisson as comfortable as he could and traveled on to Genoa, and led help back to rescue the man.

A doctor in Genoa said it was necessary to amputate Sisson's legs, but he would need chloroform and there was none in town.

Thompson set out across the Sierras for Sacramento for the anesthetic. He returned from the 280-mile trip five days later with the medicine. The gravely ill Sisson lost his feet but did survive.

For warmth, Thompson depended on a Mackinaw jacket. He carried no blankets, but did carry matches with which to light a fire.

Virginia City *Territorial Enterprise* reporter Dan de Quille wrote of Thompson: "He flew down the mountainside. He did not ride astride his pole or drag it to one side as was the practice of other snowshoers, but held it horizontally before him after the manner of a tightrope walker."

In one gesture of benevolence, Snowshoe carried a pack of needles and a chimney for a kerosene lamp so a widower, a Mrs. Franklin, could continue her winter sewing. He brought violin strings for Richard Cosser, a local fiddler.

When the first issue of the Territorial Enterprise came off the presses December 18, 1858, it was Snowshoe Thompson who carried Nevada's first newspaper to the miners.

In 1859, Thompson was asked to take an unusual blue rock that was corrupting the gold-bearing ore in a Washoe, Nevada, mine to Sacramento to have it assayed. It turned out to be rich in silver, and signaled the discovery of the famous Comstock Lode.

Thompson married an English woman named Agnes Singleton and settled on the property he had homesteaded. When not carrying mail, Snowshoe raised wheat, oats, hay and potatoes. He cared for 90 head of cattle and 20 horses, half of which he owned.

Thompson served on the Alpine County board of supervisors from 1868 to 1872, and was a delegate to the Republican State Convention in Sacramento in 1871.

Even though a number of resolutions were submitted to Congress in Washington, D.C.,

Snowshoe Thompson was never paid for his services delivering United States Mail.

He died on May 15, 1876, of appendicitis which developed into pneumonia. He and his son Arthur, who died two years later of diphtheria, were buried side-by-side in the cemetery at Genoa.

His wife Agnes placed a headstone of snow-white marble on Snowshoe's grave. A pair of crossed skis were engraved on the stone, along with the words, "Gone but not forgotten."

Chapter 36

The Chinese Tong Wars

The first Chinese tong war occurred in Weaverville in 1854. The gold mining town had a Chinese population of about 2,000. The Orientals were divided into two "companies", one of which was from Canton and the other from Hong Kong.

An argument developed between the two Chinese factions and war was declared. It was a boon for local blacksmiths because during the next several days they were swamped with orders for spears, pikes and tridents.

There was much bargaining to gain the services of weapon makers. One blacksmith agreed to make 100 spears for the Cantons at $1.50 each. Within an hour, the Hong Kongs upped the Canton bid by giving the blacksmith an order for 200 spears.

The Cantons immediately countered with an even bigger order and at a higher price. They would pay $2.50 each for 300 spears.

The two Chinese groups marched, drilled, and maneuvered up and down the city's streets. They wore tin helmets, carried iron shields, homemade bombs and squirt guns loaded with a foul-smelling liquid.

The miners watched the war preparations with glee and looked forward to the upcoming war that was set for July 4.

When the Cantons and the Hong Kongs took their positions on a field outside of town, a sheriff attempted to stop the battle. The American spectators protested, saying that many had come a long way to see this event. The sheriff allowed the activity to proceed.

One writer described the activity this way.

With much beating of gongs and tooting of horns, the two parties started their maneuvers. Now they would halt, with their poles upright looking like a forest of trees. Then lowering the points of their spears, with awful yells, they would run two or three hundred yards. Then stop, the front rank dropping on one knee, forming a perfect rampart of spears and shields.

There was some apparent collusion between some of the American spectators and the Hong Kongs. When the Hong Kongs charged, the Cantons fell back.

A reserve group of Cantons came up on the flank of the Hong Kongs. Some of the Americans joined the fray and drove the Cantons from the field, but not before eight Chinese and one American was killed, and several others wounded.

A second tong war occurred at Chinese Camp two years after the Weaverville affair. It all started when a huge stone rolled from the diggings of one group of Chinese miners into the area where other Chinese were working.

A fight ensued and when it was over, both groups sent out a call for help to their respective tongs, the Sam Yap and the Yan Wo. Each group felt it had lost face and the only proper thing to do was to hold a full-scale war between the tongs.

Each side built up a huge arsenal of crude iron weapons. Again, as in Weaverville, American blacksmiths made these weapons. Beside the pikes, spears, daggers and shields, a few firearms were brought in from San Francisco as well.

The Chinese groups hired American miners to instruct them on how to use these firearms, which were strange weapons to the Chinese.

The actual war event occurred October 25, 1856. Twelve hundred members of the Sam Yap tong met nine hundred Yan Wo tong brothers on Crimea Flat some three miles from Chinese Camp.

When the war ended, there were four dead and another four injured. American law authorities arrested two hundred and fifty others.

Chinese miners made up a considerable contingent of gold seekers. By 1852, there were eighteen thousand Chinese men and only fourteen Chinese women in California. During the next fourteen years, this number grew to a population of 116,000 Chinese.

American miners looked down upon the Chinese miners. The Chinese were not only required to pay a miner's tax which was not required of American miners, but generally forced to work abandoned mines. Their patient methods allowed them to make a living in this way.

At one point, in 1858, California lawmakers passed a law forbidding any more Chinese being brought into California. If a ship's captain was convicted of disobeying this order, he would be liable to a fine of $400 to $600, or imprisonment for up to one year.

Chinese immigrants provided important labor for a number of industries in the building of California, not the least of which was the railroads.

Index

219

About the Author

Alton Pryor

Alton Pryor has self-published fifty-plus books since turning 70 in 1997—many of them about California's past and the colorful characters who rode our trails to fame or infamy.

To date he has sold more than 180,000-plus copies of his first book, "Little Known Tales in California History", and has done respectably well with most of his other titles.

But until fate derailed his 33-year journalism career, he never aspired to write a book, and certainly never anticipated he would come to be regarded as "Mr. Self-Publishing" by his peers in the Sacramento area. 212

"I would have liked living in the Old West," he says. "I wanted, at one time, to be a really good cowboy. I had horses as a young man and even took a raw colt and trained it to work cattle."

But, by the time Pryor was born on March 19, 1927, the era of gunslingers and gold miners was over, and he started life, instead, on his family's farm outside of King City in the Salinas Valley.

He was terminated after writing for 27 years for a magazine. The magazine was sold to a midwest firm.

Pryor turned to writing books and says now, "I wish I had been fired 20 years earlier."

26504279R00126

Made in the USA
San Bernardino, CA
30 November 2015